Unbreakable Dolls, Too

True Stories of Amazing Pioneer Women

Julie McDonald

To Dennis and Susie McDonald.
Thanks for 45 years of fun, love and laughter!

About the Author

Julie McDonald is a third generation native of Flagstaff, Arizona. She is an avid gardener, selling her produce to customers at her farmstand in her neighborhood. Her first book, *Farm Your Front Yard,* is filled with creative ideas to help people garden successfully in the Inter-Mountain West. Her second book, *Unbreakable Dolls,* was to honor her grandmother, Mathilda Benson and other pioneer women of northern Arizona. *Unbreakable Dolls, Too* expands to Colorado and New Mexico as well as Arizona. Julie has four adult children and six grandchildren. Her passion is promoting the wonderful Good News of Jesus Christ.

The stories in this book are true. Some were gathered from the women themselves and some from oral histories of the women's families. Research at fine pioneer museums in Colorado, New Mexico and Arizona supplemented these stories. They represent history as seen through the eyes of the people who lived it. This book is meant to inform, inspire, and entertain. It is not intended to be used as a textbook of absolute fact.

Verner Gustav "Spud" Benson was born in Flagstaff, July 1, 1914. From a very young age he entertained family and friends with his cartoons. Whether at home, school or work (City of Flagstaff and Northern Arizona University) the cartoons brightened everyone's day! Over time he published hundreds of cartoons in numerous magazines, newspapers and periodicals. In the mid-sixties he ventured into a new arena writing dozens of humorous short stories about life in Flagstaff and Northern Arizona in "the good old days." He had many fans around the state and country but I was always his biggest fan! He was a gifted artist and writer but more importantly he was a wonderful father. He died 30 years ago in 1981. I still miss him. I joined each profile of these amazing women with one of my dad's stories that complements theirs.

ISBN 978-0-9858952-0-4

Photos
Front cover: Pearl Cromer, 1900, courtesy of the Cromer/McEuen Families
Back cover: Julie and Roxi, Courtesy Randi Diskin

Published by Julie McDonald

First Edition 2012

Contents

Introduction

Selling vegetables in my driveway at my farmstand has brought me fame, but not necessarily fortune. This feat in Flagstaff, Arizona, with its challenging growing conditions inspired my first book, "Farm Your Front Yard". I began the book with a brief synopsis of my grandmother, Mathilda Benson, a Swedish immigrant who came to Flagstaff in 1909. She has always inspired me. She was widowed when my father, Verner Benson, was only two years old. She raised all six children alone and put them through college selling vegetables that she grew on a little half-block farm in downtown Flagstaff. I was so happy that many of my readers found her story interesting. I wanted to write more about her, but her story is not enough for a whole book. As I thought about it, I began to wonder if there weren't other women like her, who had not been written about before. Not the rich and famous, which really lived much easier lives, but other immigrants, minorities, those that worked hard, faced impossible difficulties, experienced one setback after another, yet remained "Unbreakable". These women are the true unsung heroines of the West.

My first book "Unbreakable Dolls" has my grandmother's story along with seven other ordinary yet amazing women from Northern Arizona. With each story I included one of my dad's wonderful short stories about early days in Arizona which were published in the 1960's -70's. "Unbreakable Dolls, Too" has six more wonderful stories of amazing women paired with complimentary stories of my dad's. There is a wider geographical area represented in "Unbreakable Dolls, Too" with women from Colorado, New Mexico and both southern and northern Arizona. Be inspired, encouraged and challenged. Enjoy these women and my dad's fun stories!

—Julie

CHAPTER ONE

Clara Brown

1800-1885

Sketch of Clara Brown by Joe Blalock Jr., 2012

Fifty-nine year old Clara Brown slipped quietly into the shadows to watch and wait. The boat dock in Leavenworth, Kansas was teaming with people, goods and animals. Everyone, it seemed, was caught up with "gold fever" and heading west. Clara had decided to head west too. Clara wanted to make sure she got on a "good train" and the wagon master was the key. She had a sixth sense about people. She could tell if they were kind or mean, honest or dishonest, fair or unfair. After observing for two hours she finally approached a group of men and said, "If I cook and I do laundry for you, could I get passage for myself and my laundry equipment?" The men were incredulous and one said, "We don't want no old slave latchin' on to our wagon train." Ignoring him, Clara fixed her gaze on Colonel Wadsworth, the wagon master, pulled out her "Freedom Papers" and said, "I'm not a slave, I'm free. I'm a good laundress and a good cook to boot." Colonol Wadsworth had five families and 26 single men signed up for his train. A good cook and a laundress would sure come in handy. After looking over her papers he said to her, "Can you be ready in one week?"

The first night out, Clara had plenty to think about. Her instinct about Colonel Wadsworth was correct. He was a strong, powerful man, a natural leader, fair, and he knew the trail like the back of his hand. He had already settled the first controversy regarding where Clara would sleep. "Where's that Negro going to sleep, not in a wagon!" He had given Clara an oil cloth and a quilt and now Clara snuggled into her bed under the wagon.

Born a slave in 1800 she had spent the first 36 years with a kind family. Ambrose and Myra Smith treated their slaves well. Myra had taught Clara to read and write. Each Sunday, the family, including the slaves, went to church at the home of a neighbor, a farmer by the name of Valentine Cook. It was there at age 10 that Clara had an "awakening" and came to know the living God. He promised to guide and protect her. Clara spoke of it as her sure foundation of her entire life. She said later, "Darlin, I was nothing but a child when God came to me and took me to Jesus, no matter what happened I knew God would bear me up." At age 18 she met her beloved Richard with his "big smile and his big heart." They had "jumped the broom." They had four children, Richard Jr., Margaret and twin girls, Eliza Jane and Paulina Ann. Richard, Clara and their family were happy together.

> **"Jumping the Broom"**
> Since slaves were considered property, they had no legal rights nor could they legally marry. Slaves held a ceremony in which a broom was placed on the floor and the young couple literally jumped over it. In this way they pledged their love and commitment to one another.

Then back to back tragedies shattered their lives. One summer day in 1834 when the twins were 8 they had gone to the creek to go swimming after their work was done. Suddenly Eliza Jane came home screaming; Paulina Ann had gotten pulled under and had drowned. She was buried in the Smith family cemetery under the Mulberry tree. Eliza Jane sobbed through the ceremony and for days and months afterwards. She often awoke screaming with nightmares, reliving the tragedy. Clara knew it would take time for her little girl to heal.

Two years later Ambrose Smith died and the family was forced to sell everything including their slaves. Richard and Richard Jr. were sold to a man that Clara had a bad feeling about. Margaret went to another family. Little Eliza Jane in a pink pinafore trembling on the auction block was bought by yet another family. The last Clara saw of her she was riding in the back of a wagon loaded with all the other goods the family had bought that day. Clara was sold to the Brown family who lived in eastern Kentucky, in Russellville. The Brown family loved her, calling her Aunt Clara. They even helped her try and locate her family. One night God spoke to Clara; Richard and Richard Jr. had been worked to death. Clara had been correct, the new owner was a bad man. George Brown located Margaret. She seemed to be doing well, then suddenly she died of a chest ailment. There was not a trace of Eliza Jane. A family named Covington had purchased her but George Brown could not find them.

For twenty years Clara lived with the Browns caring for the three daughters as they grew up. When Mr. Brown died he left Clara 300.00. Oh my, what would she do with 300.00? Another surprise awaited her. His three daughters, Mary Prue, Lucinda and Evaline gave her the most precious gift of all, the gift of freedom! Clara was excited and scared all at the same time. For two years after she left the Browns, she worked as hired help for a German family, trying desperately to locate Eliza Jane. Now she had exhausted all the leads in the east. Maybe the family that had purchased Eliza Jane had "gold fever" like everyone else and had gone west. Clara

> A Day on the Wagon Train for Clara
>
> Rise before dawn
> Make a fire
> Roast green coffee beans
> Grind the coffee
> Fry up bacon and eggs
> Milk the cow
> With milk from the cow, make biscuits
> Feed 26 men, wash all the dishes in boiling creek water, dry and put them away
> WALK 6-8 MILES
> "Nooner", make a pot of stew for 26 men
> Use herbs found in the grasses while walking for added flavor
> Wash all the pots and pans and put away
> WALK 5-6 MILES
> Prepare dinner, a "lick skillet" of beans and any leftovers with bread and a dessert of fruit or cobbler
> Milk the cows, let the warm milk set over-night, skim the cream off in the morning and hang in the wagon. The bumpy ride would turn it into butter.
> Evening, gather buffalo chips or any stray wood for the next morning's fire. Bandage the blisters on her feet and mend the holes in her socks and shoes.
> SUNDAY a day of rest for most everyone on the train, but not Clara. Clara did laundry, sewed shirts, and hung meat to make jerky and baked bread for the week.
> Repeat for 8 weeks, 56 days

would go west and find out.

Clara was not impressed with the twin towns of Cherry Creek and Auroria, (later to be named Denver) muddy, dirty with only a few scattered buildings. Clara looked for anyone who could be Eliza Jane. With few Negros it didn't take long to determine she wasn't there. At least not yet. Clara set about advertising her services of laundry and cooking to support herself. Her life revolved around three specific goals:

1) Find Eliza Jane.

2) Help people in need. Any down and out person was a candidate, man or woman, black, white, red or yellow, any occupation. She had a special affinity for Indians, her grandmother being a full blooded Cherokee. She fed them, comforted

the lonely, and doctored the sick.

3) Prayer meetings. If Clara wasn't at one, she was hosting one. Clara had always been a part of a congregation and she was anxious to get a real church going in this rough and tumble town.

The following year Clara moved 40 miles up into the mountains to Central City. A Methodist church was going in and 15,000 miners meant a lot of soul work and a lot of laundry business. Clara hoped to make enough money to help the Methodist church get established and have enough to continue her search for Eliza Jane.

Getting to Central City was a problem. Clara, as usual had thought of a solution. Clara approached a man who had been with her on the wagon train and said, "I need help. I want to move my laundry business up to Central City. They won't let a colored person ride the stage coach. I will pay you to take me up as your servant." Plan in place, Clara put on her shabbiest calico and a worn bandana on her head. They rode the forty miles straight uphill from an elevation of 5,200 in Denver to 9,000 feet in Central City. No one guessed it was Clara who paid the fare.

Clara found a two room cabin with a woodshed. In the main room she set up her stove for heating her boiler and iron. She was happy to see that even with equipment set up for business there would still be plenty of room for prayer meetings. The second room was her bedroom. She pounded nails to hang the clothes on and piled hay on the log bed. The shed was stacked with wood for the stove and there was plenty of room on the floor for anyone who needed a place to stay. The most difficult aspect of the cabin was the outhouse. A far piece from the cabin and with a slight incline facing north, it was icy most of the year. The trail was prone to snow drifts and Clara or her guests often had to plow their way through. More than once Clara encountered bears, mountain lions and other wild animals. If Denver had been wild, Central City was ten times wilder. Gunshots rang out day and night; the mines ran 24 hours a day with dynamite blasts constantly disturbing the peace. Murders and hangings were weekly events.

Clara painted a sign and hung it outside. It simply said, LAUNDRY. Customers flocked in and Clara raised her price to 50 cents a shirt. Henry Poyntner had moved to Central City a year before Clara. A Negro handyman, he lived alone. Clara invited him to dinner and found he was the same age as Margaret, had she lived. Next were miners Jeremiah Lee

---

How to launder a miner's shirt:

You will need:

Wood fire going, two buckets, 2 laundry tubs, metal boiler tank, washboard, lye soap, water, knife, clothespins, clothespin bag, rope, wood, flat top stove, iron and STRONG MUSCLES.

String the rope from a nail on your house, wrap around a tree and back again.

Place boiler on the stove.

Fetch water from the creek in your buckets, about 12. Enough to fill the wash tub and the boiler.

Slice lye soap into thin pieces. Put into the boiler and stir until soapy.

Using an empty bucket, put the soapy water into the empty washtub. Add the shirts.

One at a time, rub the wet shirts on the washboard, concentrate on the dirtiest spots. Keep rubbing till shirts are clean.

Rinse each shirt in the rinse tub.

Wring each shirt by hand; squeeze hard to get all the water out.

Hang each damp shirt on the line.

If it is windy, use extra clothespins.

Make sure there are no clumps of fabric or the shirts won't dry.

When all the shirts are washed, dump the washtubs.

Go get more water from the creek, rinse tub and boiler.

Hang the wash board and basket in a tree to dry.

While clothes are drying, heat your iron on the stove

Take the shirts off the line and drop in the basket. Lay each shirt on a cloth on your kitchen table.

Use the heavy hot iron to press out the wrinkles.

Fold the ironed shirts and put them in your laundry basket in order of delivery.

Carry the basket on your head up and down the streets and mountain trails to your customers.

Author's note: This difficult job was made much worse without any hand protection. The water, lye and cold, dry, wind would have left Clara's hands cut and bleeding.

and Lorenzo Bowman. She took a "grubstake" in their mining ventures. She not only fed them, she prayed for their protection and their success.

Whenever Clara needed to talk to God she dropped to her knees, whether in her cabin, on the street, in a field, it didn't matter. Startled residents of Central City saw her often on her knees praying out loud for Jeremiah and Lorenzo. After a time they became accustomed to it and attributed it to "Aunt Clara's way".

Clara was a ray of sunshine in Central City. One morning at 5 a.m., a lawyer was walking up Eureka Gulch in one of his foul moods. He was astounded to hear "songs of praise and expressions of great joy". There was Clara, basket of laundry on her head, singing and clapping as she walked along, "Bless the Lord, Bless the Lord, I am so happy this morning". Right then and there this educated man knew Clara had something that he didn't have, but he wanted it. Clara told him of Jesus, his love for mankind that sent him to the cross. She invited him to her prayer meeting. He was the first member of the new Methodist church.

Clara's care of destitute miners and her growing list of grubstakes began to pay off. Most of Central City attributed her success to beginners luck but Clara called it God's grace. When a mine paid off, Clara invested the money in another mine, land or a house. After 10 years, between her interest in mines, property purchases, and her booming laundry business Clara had $10,000.00, making her one of the richest women in the West. Still Clara lived in the same two room cabin, wearing the same clothes, hanging them on the same nail. While many people flaunted their mining wealth, Clara had more important things to do with her money. She had been giving money to her church, now at 225 people; she was the single biggest contributor. She helped almost every other congregation in town as well. She continued feeding, housing and helping people and saving money to continue her hunt for Eliza Jane.

One of the many people who came knocking on Clara's door was a well-dressed Negro man from Chicago named Barney Ford. Even though he was wealthy, being a Negro he couldn't rent a hotel room or a cabin. He had heard of Clara and came for help. After her prayer meetings, Barney entertained Clara and her many friends night after night with stories of his and others escapes to freedom on the Underground Railroad. Barney had been a slave on his master's riverboat. One night, with the help of an actor on board Barney donned a dress and bonnet, some pink greasepaint and danced right off the river boat to freedom. On the Underground Railroad he had gone by foot, wagon, boat and even in a casket with holes poked in the side for air. Clara shared with Barney her desire to go back east again to look for Eliza Jane. Barney's wise counsel was, "Not yet Clara, it is not safe, if Abraham Lincoln gets elected, and I think he will, he will fight for the end of slavery. Until then, you're not safe in the East." As it turned out Barney Ford was right. When Barney gave Clara the green light she set off for Kansas. What she found there broke her heart. Negros wandering the streets, looking for their families and for work. She searched for Eliza Jane for months with no success.

One day she was so discouraged she dropped to her knees and began praying and crying. There she felt God tell her to put together a "family" of freed slaves who had no relatives. If she couldn't find her Eliza Jane then she would help these people who couldn't find their families either. In 1866 she rounded up around 25 people and arranged passage on a wagon train.

It was the same trip Clara had been on 10 years earlier but this time she rode. The residents of Central City welcomed her "family". She found every one of them jobs and put them on property or in homes she owned. She put a 1,000 reward for information on Eliza Jane and advertised in newspapers and through churches around the country.

In 1870 a tragedy was unfolding. Scoundrels in the east to "get rid of freed slaves" told them there was 40 acres and a mule for every Negro in Kansas. Clara received word that 1,000 were arriving daily. There was no land, no mule and no food. 50 a day were dying of starvation. Clara again left for Kansas, this time on the train. Clara got busy and spoon-fed the victims. Each mouth she fed, each illness she nursed, each soul she comforted, she asked, "Did you ever know an Eliza Jane?" At times a lead would seem promising only to end in disappointment.

At 80 Clara's health began to fail. Central City was too cold. A friend gave her a small house in Denver and promised she could live there for the rest of her life. "How sad," people said of Clara, "the poor old woman never found her daughter." Clara herself finally admitted she would never see her daughter this side of heaven.

Valentine's Day, 1882, a letter was delivered to Clara from her long time friend, Becky Johnson who had moved to Iowa. Becky, also a freed slave, had been instrumental in helping Clara learn the laundry business.

Dearest Clara,

I was at the post-office when I ran into a women by the name of Mrs. Brewer. Then I heard the clerk address her as Eliza Jane. Well honey, you know I had to ask! Yes, Mrs. Brewer had been in Kentucky. Yes, she remembered getting dressed up and being sold. No, she couldn't remember her mother's name; it was "Mammy". Yes she was with a family named Covington for 20 years. She married a slave named Jeb from a neighboring farm and they had nine children. Well when I asked about a sister that drowned she started crying, right there in the post office. She doesn't have money to come to Colorado but she is desperate to see you. She thought you had died in slavery long ago. My dear friend I am so happy for you,

Sincerely and affectionately,
Becky

Aunt Clara Brown had a burst of energy that defied reason; she was going to Iowa to see her daughter! She couldn't stop crying that at long last she had found her Eliza Jane. On March 9th she stepped off the train and into the arms of Eliza Jane, who had Richards "great big smile." It had been raining and the two lost their balance, slipped and fell into the mud but they didn't let go, not for a long, long time.

Eliza Jane returned with her mother to Denver where she cared for her for the last three years of her life. She got to know her friends and heard of the many lives that Clara had touched throughout the years. Clara was now old and getting weaker by the day, but she aged like an African Queen or a Cherokee Chief. A reporter wrote of her in 1885:

"She is a tall woman, very aged, yet she does not show the advance of years, save that she is toothless. She has a remarkable face, with high cheek bones, a long pointed nose and very black eyes. Her cast of features is strong and almost classical and the hair which curls above her temples is white as the snow."

In September of 1885, she was invited to the Colorado Pioneer Society banquet. The fashion of the day was suede, silk and satin. Clara wore a calico dress with a white apron and a colorful turban around her head. Her feet were so swollen she had to wear slippers, and be carried most of the way. She was the only person of color honored on that night.

One month later the end was drawing near. Clara never complained, she was always quick to see the best in every person and the best in very situation. As friends gathered at her bedside she said, "When I was a girl, I relied on his mercy and he fetched me through. My blessed Lord was crucified, think how he suffered. My little sufferings was nothing honey, and the Lord, he gave me the strength to bear up, I can't complain." On October 26, 1885 it was as if she looked into heaven and saw her own mother there to welcome her. She reached out and said, "Mammy!"

Sweet Clara Brown was home at last.

Life Facts:

Husband, Richard (last name unknown): 1798-1838
Clara Smith Brown: 1800-1885

Children:
Richard Jr. 1820-1838
Margaret: 1823-1840
Paulina Ann: 1826-1834
Eliza Jane: 1826-

Grandchildren: 9

Best recipe: Soups and stews with vegetables and whatever meat, wild or domestic, was available

Favorite quote: "Jesus will bear you up."

Passing of the Backhouse,
March 1972
Verner G. Benson

On my recent travels through Arizona it came to my attention that a charming bit of Americana has almost completely vanished from the scene. Carefully restored old homes, saloons, forts and even ancient Indian ruins are easy to discover, but the old outhouse has disappeared.

It is true that in out of the way U.S. Park Service campgrounds rude replicas have been erected. But they are sorry things, lacking in character and distinction, built out of need rather than the desire to preserve history. Constructed to government specifications and made with seven carbon copies, they are painted an unbecoming green which offends the sensibilities of older generations familiar with the natural weathering of unpainted boards. What's more, the government's creations have led a whole generation to believe that the outhouse was a crude building, thrown up in helter skelter fashion and not a true form of native art.

Not so. Construction of an outhouse formerly required great deliberation and planning. Distance from the home had to be considered. Exposure, both aesthetically and in relation to the elements, was a factor. So were proximity to other buildings, landscaping, and, above all, consideration of the prevailing winds. Old-time artisans never built a privy upwind of the house.

Site selection had to be weighed and evaluated in other ways as well. For example, one had to remember that in winter the well-worn path to the little house out back might at times be icy. This was further complicated by the fact that the path should not lead directly to its goal but rather should curve gently so it would appear to the casual observer that the user was headed for some other destination.

Generally, when planning distance from the house, the designer calculated the average miles per hour travel speed of all members of the family. Preferably, the route to the outhouse should be downhill. This would have major effect upon the ETA (Estimated Time of Arrival) and would allow for greater-than-average speed in emergencies.

Yet, the slope of the path should not be too steep when weighed against the possibility of icy footing in winter. Younger members of the family might find it advantageous to slide to their objective but older people would find such a surface too perilous. Of course, wood ashes could be sprinkled on the path to reduce the hazard.

At last, however, the perfect site was chosen and preliminary architectural planning was begun. Doors, for example, must open outwardly and, for obvious reasons, face away from the house. At this juncture more ambitious builders might consider an L-shaped wooden screen, not only to insure greater privacy, but also to break the force of chill winds.

Layout of the interior was a family decision. The number of holes to be provided, of course, was strictly a matter of status. After all, the little place had only one occupant at a time. A considerate parent would install at least one junior-sized hole for junior members of the family.

Most important was the quality of the holes, not the number of them. They were cut by hand in wide, thick boards and lovingly finished to a satiny texture. No splinters were permitted.

Lighting and ventilation were next considered and often proved to be a knotty problem. Glass windows were out of the question in the days before frosted glass was available. Then, too, ventilation was extremely important, especially in summer. In winter, though, the same adequate ventilation caused great discomfort. Perhaps that is why our embarrassed ancestors were called "hardy."

The accepted practice was to cut holes high in the side walls, back them with screens so the flies wouldn't escape, and make them no larger than six inches. The problem lay in the design. Wives usually favored exotic designs like the fleur de lis or bunches of grapes. Children cried out for crossed swords or, the bane of the astronomer, a crescent moon with a star in the center. Husbands and fathers, on the other hand, aware of their limitations as craftsmen, held out for twin, staggered diamonds. Their wishes generally prevailed.

Interiors were left unfinished, giving the place a rustic, knotty pine look much in favor today but frowned upon by some of the fastidious of olden times. A few snobs even papered one wall.

Despite the careful planning, mistakes were often made. A vagrant

wind might blow the door open if a spring closer had not been installed. Occasionally a well meaning builder would install a lock on the outside of the door. The folly of this was soon apparent for the incumbent, secure behind his locked door, would ultimately discover that retaliation worked two ways. A thwarted, would-be user might lock the door on the outside.

Hornets and wasps found the outhouse extremely attractive and often built nests in the upper reaches. Their presence naturally destroyed the peace of mind of human occupants and no expense was spared in evicting the winged warriors. This was often accomplished by burning the nests, unfortunately, most of the outhouses were tinder dry and quite often both the nest and the outhouse went up in flames, leaving whole families in dire circumstances.

The completed outhouse was a thing of utilitarian beauty and simplicity as well as a joy forever for it answered many of the needs of man. In the outhouse could be found privacy – hence the name "privy" – and for a short time the world seemed far away. It was a place to dream great dreams, to think deep thoughts, and to philosophize. It was also a library. Mail order catalogs were there to be used as reference works, although by spring they were down to the ladies' underwear section and the colored pages.

On the night of October 31st, however, no man tarried long in the little structure out back. This was an evening for spirits to be abroad. While witches presented no problem, groups of young warlocks might well turn the place over. The timid even posted friendly guards, thereby establishing the first Early Warning System.

It has always been my hope that some civic-minded organization would find a backhouse in good condition, restore it, and preserve it forever as a bit of Americana. They might even go so far as to build a roof over the entire structure as has been done with some Indian ruins out West. Indeed, such a preserved privy with its own little slot of land might well gain distinction as the smallest dedicated park in the United States. For all of the outhouse's service to mankind it would be a fitting end.

CHAPTER TWO

Sally Rooke

1841 1908

Sketch of Sally Rooke by Joe Blalock Jr., 2012

Sally Rooke drummed her fingers on her small kitchen table. She gazed out her window at the great expanse before her, Capulin Mountain, an extinct volcano was magnificent with the setting sun casting a beautiful hue. The mesas off in the distance were tinged with reds and pinks. The prairie grass was swaying gently in the breeze. She never tired of the beauty. In her hand she held a letter, which she read again for the third time. A job offer in Folsom as the telephone switchboard operator. Should she take it? She loved her homestead in this enchanted land of the New Mexico Territory and she was steadily making improvements. She had to acknowledge that aging and increasing curvature of the spine was making life a bit difficult. A job in town would be much easier and would provide her with a little extra income to buy things for the homestead.

Sally initially came only for a visit to her good friend Dr. Virginia Morgan. During her time there, Sally fell in love with the West. At age 63, Sally packed up her things from her native Iowa, moved west and took up a homestead adjoining Dr. Morgan's.

Sally rose from the table, fixed a cup of tea, and walked outside to enjoy the spectacular sunset. "And," she said out loud, "it would be nice to visit with folks in town". She mulled over all the benefits and as darkness fell she turned and went inside. She had made up her mind, she would take the job in Folsom.

Sally loved her new job! She was always cheerful and took a great interest in others, making friends with everyone in Folsom. She would inquire about their children, their animals their business, farm or ranch. People began to notice she never spoke of her life back in Iowa. What the previous 63 years had been like for Sally Rooke or what had happened to her there no one ever knew. She did confide to a friend, "I have found youth and happiness here."

August 8, 1908

Sally awoke to a gray sky and light drizzle. "Unusual for New Mexico," she thought as she headed to her job. Late that afternoon a call came from Mrs. Ben Owen, whose family ranched on the mesa 8 miles above Folsom. "Sally, it's raining hard up here, I'm seeing our little creeks rise. I'm afraid it is all headed down the dry Cimarron." "Flashflood" had not been in Sally's vocabulary in Iowa. Since her arrival three years ago in New

> ### What is a Flash Flood?
>
> Flash Floods are a deadly phenomenon of the southwestern United States. Summer monsoons can bring heavy downpours resulting in 2-3 inches of rain in a short amount of time. Rain falling on ground with little or no vegetation, or on solid rock, or in steep canyons can turn small creeks or dry washes into raging rivers very quickly. The water moves along swiftly, carrying away everything in its path. There may be little or no warning, often the sun is shining as the water may be coming from a thunderstorm as far as 50 miles away. The only warning may be a tiny trickle of muddy water before a wall of water strikes.

Mexico she had heard of their terror but never experienced one.

For two hours, Sally alone at her switchboard, worked furiously calling one subscriber, now her friends, after another. She begged and pleaded with each one to get to higher ground, "Just in case". For some, Mrs. Owen's concern was enough, for others they complied but reluctantly. Still others argued with her, "Oh Sally, it's not raining that hard, and besides, we've never had a serious flood, we'll be fine" As darkness fell a huge roar was heard and the crashing of homes and businesses as they were swept away, people screaming in terror. Sally was in a three way conversation when suddenly a bolt of lightning and then Sally's voice ceased.

Seventeen people including Sally perished in the flashflood and most of the town was destroyed. The death toll would have been much higher had Sally not stayed at her switchboard to give warning. Sally's body was discovered seven months later several miles downstream, identified only by the curvature of the spine. A search was conducted in Iowa but no relatives came forward to claim her. She was buried in the cemetery in an un-marked grave.

July 1925

A story about Sally Rookes' heroic death 18 years earlier and the sad state of her unmarked grave appeared in the Monitor. The Monitor was a newsletter distributed throughout the Mountain States Telephone Company. The article suggested her co-workers might like to contribute a dime a piece to erect a proper granite tombstone. Nearly 5,000 contributions poured in, not only from employees of the Mountain States but from around the country. In May of the following year, a service was planned for the unveiling of the monument. People came from far and near with a delegation coming all the way by train from Denver. People were eager to share their story of how Sally's call had saved them or a loved one from the flood. Some shared how loved ones would have been spared had they only heeded Sally's warning. It seemed everyone there had a tale to tell. For the first time people realized the great impact Sally had and just how many lives she had saved. A tribute by J.E. MacDonald stated, "Indeed, if we remember that she was no longer young, that she was alone, that it was night time and that she was contending with one of nature's most terrible forces, her strength of heart and purpose were superlative."

A contributor from Boston expressed this beautiful thought:

Love not duty: For it was not her sense of duty that held her there but love for her fellow-man. Such heroism and such devotion are the clear white lights which brighten the path of life and increase our faith. Would that we all might have as glorious a passing.

The Corner Grocery, March 1973
Verner G. Benson

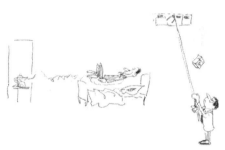

I was recently snatched from the arms of Morpheus by the smell of fresh coffee. As I lay there, drowsing, I was suddenly transported back to the old corner grocery store.

Our neighborhood had a very special grocery, and larger than ordinary, too, for it was originally built as a saloon. Prohibition, however, arrived before its completion and the owner sadly converted the building to a grocery store. This proved to be a profitable business but the owner never fully recovered from the blow and was, at times, steeped in melancholia and beer, both of his own making.

It was a strongly built building with heavy timbers and thick plank floors. It had to be, for it if had been used for its original purpose the lumberjacks of the period would have happily torn a lesser building down. A wide, low porch ran along the sides of the building. It was wide to provide shade for sleeping drunks and low to discourage cowboys from riding horses inside.

The main room was long with extremely high ceilings. Elaborate plans had been made for balconies. Where the bar had originally been scheduled a long counter had been built, complete with bins in the back containing beans, rice and other dried foods. A thin glass-covered case in front of each bin held a sample of what the bin contained and also a few unlucky insects. Back of the counter shelves had been built all the way to the ceiling. Canned goods reposed on the lower shelves while boxes of cereal occupied the top shelves. To reach the cereal boxes the clerk used a long pole armed with clamps which could be operated from the bottom. The clamps often slipped and the box of cereal would fall, striking the clerk on the head. It is quite easy to understand why boxes of cereal were stored there and not stacks of cement or iron pots.

To reach the canned goods on the higher shelves a ladder, running on rails attached top and bottom, had been installed. It was a smooth running device and convenient, but transient clerks would often attempt to mount it in the same manner one swings aboard a moving freight car. Used in this cavalier fashion the ladder would often rebel, become dislodged from the bottom rail, and throw the clerk heavily to the floor. Bandaged clerks were often to be seen swinging aboard a passing freight, muttering.

Lying in wait at the front of the store was the candy counter, viewed through impenetrable glass. Originally the candy had been of different types, hard, soft and medium but years of neglect and the dry air of Arizona had now given it all the consistency of stone. This mattered little to the neighborhood urchins for they knew all too well soft candy was gone in a twinkling. Not so this candy, for a Cherinut, properly aged, could be gnawed on for days.

At the other end of the long counter, safely away from the occasional impressionable piece of candy, lay the cheese. This was a full sized cheese, weighing possibly a hundred pounds, set upon a turning, circular platform. A heavy cutting knife swung from the center

of the platform and by turning the platform the required distance a wedge of cheese, approximately one pound, was sheared off. I have always suspected the mechanism of this one had been tampered with for the owner always slapped a piece of paper on the scale before weighing the cheese. While this was presumably for sanitary reasons, it was unusually heavy paper, any germ would have been crushed, and most patrons left with three quarters of a pound of cheese and one quarter pound of paper.

Other types of cheese were carried but these were confined to a heavy wooden box fastened with a heavy hasp. This was powerful cheese and the owner always stood back and reached in gingerly, as though they might attack him. He was well advised to do this, for the fumes alone had been known to flatten a spinster and curl up a child or two.

Across from the cheese area a small butcher shop had been constructed. The entire area had been screened off but it was always a matter of conjecture whether this was to keep the flies out or in. I shall never forget the scale in the butcher shop for it bore the legend "onest Weight – No Springs." In later years people told me it probably read "Honest Weight – No Springs." Possibly the "H" was often obscured by a thumb.

Across from the long counter a variety of hardware items were displayed openly: wash tubs, copper boilers, mops and brooms. This open display indicated no trust in the customer. The items were carefully chosen and would not fit comfortably in the largest pocket. It might have been possible to shoplift a wash tub but it would have required professional talent and an unusual fence.

Strongest of all memories, however, are the odors of the long-ago store. Fondly recalled are the pungent smell of fresh ground coffee, the omnipotent cheese and a thousand other tantalizing but unidentified odors. The modern supermarket has much to offer: variety, canned music, a lack of dogs and easily available merchandise for the dishonest. But the only smells are those of disinfectant. Even limburger has been deodorized.

CHAPTER THREE

Mary Ann
Tewksbury
Rhodes
1865-1952

Mary Ann kept one eye on the clothespins and the other eye on the top of the hill. She was taking down the laundry on a beautiful fall day in Globe in the Arizona Territory but her mind was not on the laundry. Her hands were sweaty and her heart was pounding. She knew this day had great significance. JD Tewksbury was coming again to call on her mother, and this time he was bringing his sons with him. Mary Ann knew that could mean only one thing. An announcement of an upcoming marriage would most likely be made. This would be her mother Lydia's third marriage. Mary Ann Crigger's father had died when she was young. Her mother remarried John Shultes and he had also died, leaving two sons he had with Lydia. Mary Ann was happy for her mother as life had been so difficult. JD was a nice man and she liked him. Oh, but there was lots of talk in town about the good looking Tewksbury boys. Mary Ann had yet to see any of them but her friends had and they had been quick to tell her, "Oh Mary Ann, they are just so handsome, every one of them." Another friend added, "You know they are half Indian, on their mother's side, she was a real beauty they say, died a while back of consumption. Left 5 kids, 4 boys and a girl." Not only were they good looking but a bit flamboyant and a little on the reckless side.

"They are coming Mama!" Mary Ann shouted to her mother as she grabbed the last item of clothing off the line and rushed in the house. She looked aghast at her brothers, "I just cleaned you up, how did you manage to get so dirty?" Thomas the oldest responded, "Playing with the chickens." She grabbed them both and quickly cleaned face and hands. Mary Ann saved the lecture about bothering the chickens that she frequently gave them and went to the front window to watch the wagon arrive. She smoothed back her black hair, untied her apron and quickly pinched her delicate ivory cheeks to add a little color. Watching from the window she quickly surveyed the wagon full of young men and made a swift assessment. The rumors about the good looking Tewksbury boys had not been exaggerated

Mary Ann watched as the Tewksbury family approached their small home. All were well groomed and in their Sunday best. Mary Ann felt her face flush bright red. "There was no need to pinch my cheeks," she thought to herself. Introductions were made then Mary Ann quickly excused herself to prepare the plates of cookies and cakes that had been prepared for company. It wasn't long before the announcement Mary Ann had been anticipating was made. James Deming (JD) Tewksbury arose and stood before the fireplace, "I have asked Mrs. Lydia Shultes to marry me and she has accepted. The wedding will be this Saturday, November 6th." Mary Ann's mind whirled as she thought of all that needed to be done in less than a week. Her first thought, "I have nothing to wear!" At 15, her finest dress was too small and threadbare. After a big evening meal was enjoyed by all, the Tewksbury's departed and Gus and Thomas were put to bed. Lydia and Mary Ann sat down to talk of all that needed to be done. Lydia smiled at her daughter and said, "Mary Ann, you have been a help to me, with losing two husbands and all. You've cared for Thomas and Gus while I worked at the boarding house. You have helped wash and iron all the laundry I have taken in. You have worked without complaint. I hope life will be a little easier." Lydia continued, "We won't be moving to Pleasant Valley until spring. The boys will be working to build fences and a barn and work on getting us a house built when they can. We will stay in Tempe and you will be able to go to school." Mary Ann jumped up and hugged her mother and said, "Oh school, that will be wonderful." Lydia added, "I know you don't have anything to wear to the wedding so I made something for you." Lydia produced a box and Mary Ann gasped when she opened it and saw a blue gingham dress with white eyelet and pearl buttons. Mary Ann held it up and Lydia said, "You will look so pretty, it matches your blue eyes. This is a gift from Mr. Tewskbury, some money to buy a new hat."

Territorial Expositor
November 6, 1879

Mr. J.D. Tewksbury was married at 4 o'clock p.m. yesterday to Mrs. Lydia Shultes. The ceremony was performed by Justice H. Dunham. After the wedding, the company partook of a fine repast, and then adjourned to the schoolhouse where dancing was kept up until midnight. *The Expositor* man got in the fun about 8 o'clock and the way he made that school house floor quake was something new to Tempe's terpsichorean bands.

The wedding day arrived with perfect weather. Lydia at 30 was attractive and youthful with JD at 55 looking handsome and distinguished. Mary Ann met the only Tewskbury girl, Elvira. Elvira was dressed in a yellow dress with yellow ribbons in her jet black hair. "Elvira looks pleased as punch", thought Mary Ann. No wonder, after caring for her father and four brothers, Elvira was ready to relinquish her duties to Lydia.

Stunning and confident in her new dress and simple white hat, the Tewksbury boys still caused Mary Ann to blush. None were tall but they were dashing and had an air of self-confidence. At the wedding dance, Mary Ann watched as the oldest, 23 year old John spoke seriously with his three younger brothers. John was about to make his intentions for Mary Ann known. He was prepared to take on anyone –all of Arizona and especially the raucous mining town of Globe– but he would start with his wild brothers. With that taken care of, John asked Mary Ann to dance.

The first winter passed quickly. Mary Ann loved going to school. Frank, the youngest was the same age as Mary Ann and they attended Tempe High School together. Lydia enjoyed her new sons, taking them fishing and teaching the older boys to read and write. None of the Tewksbury boys had any formal schooling but they were all very bright and learned quickly. In January, the whole family traveled to Phoenix for the wedding of Elvira to Henry Slosser. With the older boys working in Pleasant Valley or along Tonto basin or the Salt River, Mary Ann saw them infrequently. Whenever they did come to Tempe, John always brought Mary Ann a present, a pretty stone, a carving or a skin. Mary Ann eagerly looked

Most of the men pictured were soon to be involved in one way or another in the Pleasant Valley War. Standing: Ed Tewksbury, George Wilson, Charlie Meadows, Tom Horn, Jim Tewksbury. Kneeling: John Rhodes, Carter Hazelton, Jim Roberts, Jim Houck. 1884. Courtesy of Gila County Historical Museum.

forward to the time they would all be together in Pleasant Valley. The Tewksbury's had filed a claim in Pleasant Valley where they had constructed some rough buildings. They went to work in earnest to build a ranch house suitable for the women. The Tewksbury men were famous in the West for their fine ranch horses. They had been breeding, raising and racing horses for many years. In late April, with the snow disappearing from the rim the family began the 75 mile trek to Pleasant Valley. The trail started at the desert floor where cactus were in bloom. The ground was a carpet of new green grass with a profusion of desert flowers, yellow poppies, blue lupine and pink owl clover were just a few of the flowers they enjoyed. As they climbed the hill the cactus gave way to cedars, junipers and oak. The view of the mountains in the distance and the Salt River below was breathtaking. At night crickets chirped and coyotes howled, an occasional mountain lion was heard. The night sky was filled with millions of stars. The two week trip flew by for Mary Ann. True, it was beautiful by day and by night. Most of the time Mary Ann rode with John on his horse laughing and talking. Most of the stars were in Mary Ann's eyes as she fell head over heels in love with John Tewksbury.

Pleasant Valley was aptly named. Nestled in between two ridges with miles and miles of grassland and Cherry Creek flowed year round. At 5,200 feet it was an ideal climate for raising a variety of fruit trees and vegetables. The men set about improving the buildings and tending the horses. As with most pioneering families the Tewksbury's raised a variety of animals, cattle and hogs. "Families did whatever they could to survive" said great grandson Bill Brown. Lydia had loved gardening from her days as a young girl in Wales. She brought cuttings from her rose in Globe, some iris and numerous fruit trees. She hoped that the Freestone peach saplings she brought with her would grow. She and Mary Ann set about planting them. The romance between John and Mary Ann deepened and they often talked of marriage even though Mary Ann was barely 16 and John 24. Life in Pleasant Valley was idyllic.

On March 18, 1882 John and Mary Ann were married in Mesa, Arizona. Mary Ann was 17 and John was 25. Mary Ann found herself not only living with John but his three brothers as well. There was great haste to build John and Mary Ann their own cabin.

Lydia and Mary Ann often shared cooking duties, especially after the arrival of young Parker in 1881 to Lydia and JD. Lydia and Mary Ann noticed the "men folk" talk had changed these past few months. Instead of Apaches, mountain lions and bears the conversation was dominated with the rising tension with the Graham brothers and others who were interested in capitalizing on the valley. The Grahams had been invited to Pleasant Valley by the Tewksburys and were building a herd of cattle together. They had also helped build each other's cabins. Now the escalating tensions over cattle rustling had led to confrontations, threats and accusations. The law, in the form of the Sheriff, had come all the way from Prescott. Complaints were filed by both sides leading to numerous trips to Prescott, 90 miles away. One such trip resulted in the death of the youngest brother Frank, age 20 from pneumonia related to the arduous journey to Prescott to testify. A sheepherder hired by the Tewksbury's had been killed and retaliation quickly followed.

In the midst of this, both Mary Ann and Lydia gave birth to babies in 1884. Lydia and JD had yet another son whom they named Walter. Mary Ann and John rejoiced over a baby girl they named Bertha.

By the summer of 1887 the feud had reached a fevered pitch. John, fearful for his pregnant wife and 3 year old Bertha moved them to JD and Lydia's home. A neighbor and friend, Bill Jacobs cabin had been burned to the ground and he was also living with the family.

September 2, 1887

Mary Ann awoke early. At 8 months pregnant it was uncomfortable to sleep. Besides, there was a whole day of canning planned. Lydia's fruit trees had produced the best harvest yet. Even if there was war in the valley, women still had work to do. Their friend Sara Crouch, a schoolteacher, had come to the house and was planning on giving the women a helping hand. John and Bill Jacobs left early to care for some horses. Suddenly, shots rang out. The women were terrified. This was too close! The women couldn't see anything but the shots had come from the direction of where John and Bill were walking. As they looked out a window, shots were fired at the house. Bertha was crying uncontrollably. John Rhodes, a loyal Tewksbury friend was the only man at the house. JD had taken Gus Shultes, age 10, to Prescott the day before. Thomas, age 12 was frozen outside near the corral, unsure what to do. The seize lasted over a week. In the midst of it Mary Ann could stand it no longer. Confident they wouldn't shoot a pregnant woman she began to look for the body of her husband. Finally, after searching many hours she found both Bill and John. Bill was shot in the back, John had been shot in the neck. Clumps of hair were gripped in John's hands, the pain had been so intense. John's skull had been smashed with rocks. To add to the horror, hogs had been ravaging the bodies. Tom Graham rode up to Mary Ann on his horse. Mary Ann pleaded with him, "Let us bury them, please." Tom replied, "No Mary Ann, go back to the house." Mary Ann returned to the house, gathered some sheets and went back and covered the bodies as best she could, holding down the sheets with rocks. As she got up, sobbing over her beloved John she directed a glare at Tom Graham that caused him to turn away. With the people pinned in the cabin and apparently no help coming, John Rhodes determined to slip away and ride for help. Days later he returned with a posse and the Sheriff. One of the most famous gunfights in the history of the American West was the result as they tracked the killers 100 miles east to Holbrook.

One month later on October 3rd 1887, Mary Ann gave birth to a baby boy she named John. That long winter of 1887-1888, Mary Ann battled grief, fear, and anger. She had a three year

Tewksbury original ranch house in Pleasant Valley built in the late 1870's. Courtesy of Gila County Historical Museum.

old girl and a baby boy. She had meals to fix and work to do. She wondered when the killing would end. Most every lonely night Mary Ann cried herself to sleep.

In the late summer of 1888, John Rhodes had his own predicament. His Mexican "girlfriend" Trinidad Lopez (she refused to marry him because she had a husband in Mexico) decided she had enough of the killings in Pleasant Valley and returned to Mexico where it was safer. She went alone, leaving John with their three young children, including a very young baby. John asked Mary Ann if she would care for the baby. Mary Ann was happy to help. John Rhodes had proved to be a loyal friend to the family and had helped her since her husband's death. On December 20, 1888, John Rhodes married Mary Ann in Pleasant Valley. At the time of their marriage they had a four year old, a three year old, a two year old, a one year old and a baby. They moved into a newly completed rock house which remains today in Pleasant Valley. John brought along a young Mexican girl who had been their house help and she proved to be a great help with cooking, cleaning and caring for the children. Less than a year later a new baby arrived, only to die at birth. John and Mary Ann named her May.

In 1892, Tom Graham, who had moved to Tempe, was shot in the back while delivering a load of grain to the Hayden flour mill. Ed Tewksbury and John Rhodes were accused of the killing. "Impossible!" said witnesses. "Ed Tewskbury was seen the day before by many people seventy-five miles away in Pleasant Valley. He was home again the next day." But other witnesses claimed to have seen his great legendary stallion, Sockwad, numerous places between Pleasant Valley and Tempe. At the inquest, Annie Graham, Tom's distraught widow brought a pistol to kill Ed Tewksbury and John Rhodes. As she pulled it out, it caught on her dress and before she had a chance to fire at point blank range she was subdued and removed from the courtroom. John was released immediately and returned to Mary Ann and the children now including Ella, age one and Anna just 6 weeks. Mary Ann cried for joy, how could she bear losing another husband? Interestingly enough one of the many people to testify on behalf of John Rhodes was Raphael Lopez, the brother of Trinidad Lopez.

Ed Tewskbury spent some time in prison but was finally released after a technicality in the first trial and a hung jury in the second trial. Ed Tewskbury married Braulia Lopez and in four years they had four children. Ed was the widely respected sheriff of Globe until his untimely death in 1904. He succumbed to the same disease that had plagued his family, tuberculosis.

Josephina (Clara) Rhodes, age 18. 1904, was said to be the "spitting image" of her mother, Trinidad Lopez. Courtesy of Gila County Historical Museum.

One day, John and Mary Ann went to visit a family that needed their assistance. They would be gone all day. "Boys, do all the chores with the animals, Clara and Bertha, you are in charge of the young'uns." John spoke to the younger children, "You mind them you understand?" Clara decided to make bread for the family. Wouldn't her mother and father be so proud of her when they came home and there was fresh baked bread for the family to enjoy? ? Clara set about the task of making the bread. She had helped Mary Ann often and knew what to do. For some reason though, things weren't working out. The bread didn't rise; it just sat there in a lump. Clara thought, "Maybe I need a bit more yeast and

Top row: Clara, Ella, John T. Rhodes, Frank, Bertha. Bottom row: Mary, Mary Ann, Ora, John Rhodes, Charlie and Nan. Courtesy of Perkins Store Museum, Young, AZ.

John Tewksbury Rhodes, age 18. Courtesy of Perkins Store Museum, Young, AZ.

flour." Adding more of both, nothing happened. Clara was so disappointed. She certainly didn't want her parents to see this failure so she got a shovel, dug a hole in the front yard and put the lifeless lump in the hole and covered it up. Late in the afternoon John and Mary Ann arrived home in the wagon and were astounded to see what appeared to be a large white mushroom emerging from the ground in the front yard. Clara and the rest of the children came out of the house to meet them Clara was horrified to see what had happened. The family got years of enjoyment at Clara's expense!

Something the Rhodes family and all residents of Pleasant Valley looked forward to was the arrival of the wagon train that brought supplies from Holbrook. The wagon only came to Pleasant Valley every six months. The children would know the approximate date of arrival and wait anxiously eyes fixed on the distant hills. Finally a wisp of dust would emerge and everyone knew that was the mules kicking up dust along the trail. The cry went out, "The wagon train is coming!" Great preparations began with all the women cooking up food, using up things liberally knowing more was on the way. When the wagon arrived everyone eagerly got the items they had ordered six months earlier. Sometimes the wagon drivers brought a treat for the children, hard candy or some fruit. The homesteaders then sold or traded items to be sent back to Holbrook. They also had a list prepared for the drivers for what they needed six months down the road. Much thought had to be put into these lists if the families were going to survive and thrive. Mary Ann always made sure her order for cloth, and any sewing supplies was ready to go on the return trip. She was an excellent seamstress and made all the families clothing. In the evening a big feast was held for everyone, including the drivers on the wagon train and there was dancing till dawn and a bit of liquor was consumed.

The family moved away from Pleasant Valley in the early 1900's. John worked on a ranch near Mammoth and also along the border. In 1906 and 1907 John served as an Arizona Ranger. In 1907, when their youngest, Mary, was 9 years old, John and Mary Ann, age 43 had another baby girl, Ola. Being so much younger than the other children she was adored and doted on. It was that same year that typhoid struck the region and the whole family took ill. All the family recovered except Ola, who died at 2 months.

In 1918, the Spanish Flu struck taking fifty-million lives, a conservative number. Ora, working as an army nurse in World War I contracted the disease and died at age 23.

John's health began to decline and in 1919 at age 68, John Rhodes died. Mary Ann took a job in Phoenix managing an apartment complex. Grandchildren were also coming at a rapid rate! Bertha and Clara married brothers, George and Harry Acton. In 1930, the Depression was making life difficult for everyone. Nan and Clara and their families had moved across the street from each other in Hayden, Arizona a mining town. While Nan worked

Mary Ann Tewksbury Rhodes circa 1930's. Courtesy of Perkins Store Museum, Young, Arizona.

as a nurse, Mary Ann cared for Nan's two daughters, Mary, age 10 and Dianne, a new born, whom Mary Ann helped deliver. Bertha and her four children were not far away in Florence. With Clara's seven children, Bertha's four and Nan's two, there was lots of fun for all the cousins. Mary Ann enjoyed having more than half of her grandchildren so close. Mary

Ann went to Los Angeles often to see her daughter Ella who was a professional seamstress. Ella had learned her skills from her mother and was very gifted. A woman could come into Ella's shop, tell her what she wanted and Ella was able to custom make the garment, which always fit to perfection. Although they didn't see him much the family kept up with the success of John Tewksbury Rhodes, who was a champion rodeo performer. He had six world championship calf-roping events under his belt and when he didn't win the championship it was usually because he had been beaten by his son, Tommy Rhodes. The two teamed up together to win team-roping in 1936 and 1938, the only father son combo to have achieved such an honor.

In 1952, Mary Ann was on her way to visit a grandson when she fell in Shamrock, Texas and broke her hip. Two months later, on Christmas Eve at age 88 she died. Mary Ann Crigger Tewksbury Rhodes had lived a life like no other. Her life and those she loved had played out in books, movies, documentaries, Arizona and United States History. It was a life filled with tragedies, losses, and drama. Through it all, she was a lovely, compassionate, caring woman living life as she had always done- never slipping into bitterness or anger, but being thankful to God, for along with the tragedies had come many blessings.

Epilogue

So who killed Tom Graham? Mary Ann's children wanted to know what really happened. Late in life Mary Ann finally told one of her sons, "Uncle Ed killed Tom Graham to keep Papa (John Rhodes) from doing it." Ed Tewksbury had several horses lined up in a route and did manage to ride 150 miles in two days, an epic feat. How did they get away with it? Frontier Justice and the Tewksbury's had a lot of friends.

Life Facts:
John Tewksbury 1856-1887 (31)
John Rhodes 1851-1919 (68)
Mary Ann Tewksbury Rhodes 1864-1952 (86)

Children:
Bertha Tewksbury Rhodes 1884-1967
John "Frank" Rhodes (mother, Trinidad) 1885-1911
Josephina "Clara" Rhodes (mother, Trinidad) 1886-
John Tewksbury Rhodes 1887-1965
William "Billy" Rhodes (mother, Trinidad) 1888-
May Rhodes 1889, died at birth
Ella Rhodes 1890-
Anna "Nan" Rhodes 1892-
Ora Rhodes 1895-1918, died of the Spanish Flu
Charlie Rhodes 1896-
Ola Rhodes 1907, died at 2 months of Typhoid fever

23 grandchildren
31 great-grandchildren

Best recipe: breads of all kinds and Mexican food

Jim Ellison and Bertha Tewksbury Rhodes Acton at the grave of Bertha's father, John Tewksbury.

Pleasant Valley, even today is extremely isolated. Located on the rugged Mogollon Rim, mountains, steep canyons and dense forests make the area even now a formidable place. Pleasant Valley was 70 miles from Globe, 70 miles from Holbrook and 90 miles from Prescott, as the crow flies, but they weren't flying, they traveled over hard and difficult trails, on horses or wagons making the journey much more difficult. The Tewksbury family staked a claim on land in Pleasant Valley in 1878. A short time later while in Globe, John Tewksbury invited the Graham brothers to Pleasant Valley. There was plenty of land, grass as far as the eye could see and a steady supply of fresh water. It would be nice to have neighbors. The Tewksburys and the Grahams were friends, helping one another build their cabins. They also went in together to form a joint herd of cattle. When the Grahams tried to persuade the Tewskburys to rustle cattle from other settlers in the area, the Tewksburys refused, saying they wouldn't steal from their neighbors. This created tension between the two families but they continued to build the herd of cattle and forged a brand together. Tom Graham and John Tewksbury were going to Prescott to register the brand. Prescott was 90 miles away, a long, arduous journey even today. In the late 1800's it took several days, one way. John Graham told them he had to go to Prescott anyway, he would be happy to register the brand for them and save them the trip. In Prescott, the Territorial Capital, John Graham registered the brand in the Graham name ONLY. He effectively rustled the Tewskbury share of cattle right out from under them. The Pleasant Valley War was on! Murders, lynchings, vigilante groups, posses, inquests, trials and juries became all to familiar to the residents of Pleasant Valley. It became a terrifying place to live. Lawmen from every direction were involved, such notables as Commodore Perry Owens, Sheriff of Apache County, Sheriff Mulvenon of Prescott and William "Bucky" O'Neil. Men disappeared, their bodies never found. Men were found murdered on the trails leading in and out of Pleasant Valley, no one knew who they were or if it was related to the war. Prized animals were also killed. It was America's most deadly feud, far surpassing the more well known "Hatfield and McCoy" feud, lasting more than a decade. It is often reported as a cattle vs. sheep range war, but the Tewksburys took sheep on shares two years after the feud began, an aggravating factor, but not the cause of the feud. The exact death toll will never be known, the best estimates are between 20 and 30. It devastated not only the Tewksburys and the Grahams but many other families as well. No women were killed, but they were still victims, losing husbands, fathers and sons. Numerous books have been written and then made for television. In 1992, the movie, "Gunsmoke, to the Last Man" is a depiction of the Pleasant Valley War.

The Territorial Papers, January 1972
Verner Benson

Author's Note: The story my dad wrote in 1972 fits perfectly with the story I'm writing in 2012, 40 years later. The newspapers played an integral role, fanning the fire in the Pleasant Valley War. Small, struggling newspapers competing for readers used the Pleasant Valley War as fodder to gain market share. While talking with Bill Brown, Mary Ann's great grandson, he elaborated, "No one in Arizona was neutral including the newspapers. The papers took sides and it was evident in the first paragraph whose side they were on. Those dastardly Tewkburys or those interloping Grahams."

Early Arizonans saw little hope for the cultivation of the soil. Cactus did quite well in southern areas and pines and potatoes could be grown in the northern areas. One thing did flourish: newspapers. No town seemed too tiny to support them. If the inhabitants were illiterate the papers could be used for wallpaper.

The first Arizona newspaper was published in Tubac in the spring of 1859. Tubac hardly seemed to be the center of culture. According to all reports, its population at the time consisted mostly of rowdies from Sonora, Texans who had left their native state hurriedly and in darkness, and a scattering of horse thieves. These were apparently literate horse thieves, for the paper was an immediate success. It was called The Weekly Arizonian and true to its name was published once a week but not necessarily on the same day.

The press it was printed on was shipped around the Horn, where it heard a good deal of rough talk, and laboriously freighted from California to Tubac. It was a Washington hand press and as tough as the editors who used it. Its arrival in Tubac was greeted with cheers. Some of the comments it printed were not. Nearly twenty years later it arrived in Tucson to belabor the citizens via the Tucson Star. Still operating, and the object of much profanity and an occasional .44 slug, it carried its message to the peaceful citizens of Tombstone in The Nugget. Still later it carried news of socials and teas held in the Oriental and Crystal Palace saloons in the Tombstone Epitaph.

The Arizonian itself moved from Tubac to Tucson, grew bored and moved to Prescott, found Prescott dull returned to Tucson. It was not a quiet paper. While the Arizonian was quite happy to lay in wait for just about anybody or anything no issue was complete without a disparaging comment about Washington or Congress. The Arizonian spoke up for military protection for Arizona and was often in need of protection itself. It spoke up loudly for separate territorial governments for Arizona and New Mexico. New Mexico officials, reading the editorial pages, agreed with this and looked around for an ax.

Editors of these early blooming papers were a special breed and outspoken to the point of foolhardiness. The citizenry often took umbrage and the baseball bat and the pick handle were as much a part of the tools of a working editor as the freshly sharpened blue pencil. The Tombstone Epitaph happily suggested that the marshal, a man noted for his knowledge and handling of ordinance, was unable to apprehend hold-up men, not because of their cunning but because they were close personal friends. Its editorial pages also bristled with disparaging remarks about the government, Congress, outstanding and popular generals and the military establishment as a whole.

Not only did the early editors have to contend with gun-toting subscribers but also shortages of equipment and a harsh land. Communications were poor and the few lines open were strung casually from cactus to cactus. Indians found this wire made attractive ornaments and unfeeling teamsters often carried away chunks of it to effect emergency repairs. Paper was difficult to obtain and butcher paper was often used in an emergency. They rose to meet these hardships magnificently. Judge A. H. Hackney, founder of the Daily Arizona Silver Belt, found he lacked type large enough to print the masthead. The judge carved one from an ox yoke. It held up for years though it had a somewhat grainy appearance.

While the editors considered the news sacred, they considered the editorial pages their own and used them accordingly. An early editorial in the Arizonian endorsed the whiskey advertisement on the back page of the paper, commenting that the whiskey spoke with its own authority. A competing journalist hopped on this with glee, commenting that a story on an Apache raid in the Arizonian could not be relied on due to the fact that at the time of the raid the editor was closeted with the authorities and would have been unable to tell an Apache from a New York alderman.

The saloon provided a haven for early newspapermen. There is no record of a newspaper being established in Arizona until a saloon had been built and was in operation. The saloon, to early editors, provided a source of news and nourishment. This sometimes caused trouble. The editor of the Tombstone Prospector, secure in the freedom of the press and heavily laced with redeye, found himself jailed for contempt of court. He was furious.

The jailer, however, was also a firm believer in freedom of the press and had often drunk to it with the editor. Appropriate quarters were set up and the editor continued publication at the taxpayers' expense. Years later the judge who dispensed justice to the editor found himself, while practicing law, also sentenced to jail. Friends sent in liquid gifts but the judge remained despondent. When a telegram arrived the judge was beside himself with joy, believing this to be the first of a flood of messages demanding his release. Tearing it open in haste the judge found beside his name and the address of the jail the telegram contained only four words, "Are You There, Moriarity?" It was signed by his friend the editor.

The downfall of the "Baron of Arizona" was brought about by a newspaper. In 1887 James Addison Reavis laid claim to a tract of Arizona 236 miles long and 78 miles wide. Reavis based his claim on an ancient Spanish land grant held by his wife. To support his claim Reavis produced a bushel of ancient Spanish documents. The resulting outcry was heard in Pittsburgh. Editor Tom Weedin of the Florence Citizen entered the resulting fray, contending that Reavis was a fake and might even be a Republican. His shouts of disapproval were nearly drowned out when Robert G. Ingersoll, a great lawyer and wise in things legal, pronounced the claim flawless. Then Weedin's stammering and bashful printer brought down the baron's paper kingdom. On a trip to Phoenix, the printer sought out an exhibition of the baron's famous papers. On close examination Bill discovered an ancient document printed on a type of paper invented only a few years before the claim was filed. Further examination discovered an ancient Spanish document which plainly bore the water mark of a Wisconsin paper mill. Weedin was vindicated and the baron incarcerated.

Newspapers have changed. Editors are suave now, and occasionally wear ties, like at the Arizona Newspaper Association convention in Scottsdale next weekend. But most changes are on the outside. Newspapers are owned by individuals but editors seldom are. If you don't believe that, call your local editor and try to tell him what to print.

CHAPTER FOUR

*P*earl Cromer
1884-1982

Pearl Cromer, age 16, 1900. Courtesy of Cromer Family.

*F*ive year old Pearl McEuen leaned against the frame of the covered wagon gently stroking the head of her little sister, Lottie, hoping she would drift off to sleep. "How could anyone sleep with the racket her brothers were making?" She thought. "Virgil, put the stick down and leave your brothers alone!" With that welcome admonition from her father there would be peace and quiet, even though Pearl knew it would be temporary.

Emotions were running high for the McEuen family for tomorrow was moving day. The family, consisting of father and mother, Felix and Sarah and their 5 children, 3 boys and two girls with a baby on the way, would be making their second attempt to move from Texas to the Arizona Territory. Six years earlier the trip had ended in disaster. The family had made it as far as the Sacramento Mountains in New Mexico when a snowstorm had stranded them. The harsh winter that followed killed all of the cattle they had brought with them as the animals froze to death. Pearl had been born in Weed, New Mexico during that difficult time in the covered wagon. It had not only been her birth-place but the only home she had ever known. Forced to return to Texas and with no money or land the family of 7 had been living in the covered wagon for 5 years.

Felix had been working hard as a ranch hand to scrape together enough money to buy a small herd. It was slow going, but little by little the savings grew. Tomorrow the adventure would begin again. Saying good-bye to friends in Camp San Saba was difficult and tears were abundant. It was es-

Felix and Sarah McEuen taken at Madisonville, KY, 1885. Courtesy of the Cromer/McEuen famlies.

pecially hard for Sarah to say goodbye to her many friends and the help and support they had been to her. Those same women had little girls that Pearl had played with and how she was going to miss them! Although it was not stated, everyone knew they most likely would never see one another again.

The McEuens were accompanied by Sarah's family, the Sanders, who also hoped to obtain a ranch and a herd of cattle. It took the families two months to cross Texas and New Mexico. The excitement had long gone out of the trip and day after grueling hot day they walked or rode. Sarah had left Texas expecting her 7th child. Their oldest son, Jody, had died when he was just six years old. Sarah was desperately hoping they could be settled when the baby was born. But Amos Felix was born in the covered wagon in the isolated and rugged Chiricahua Mountains in the southeastern portion of the Arizona Territory.

The dream of the ranch was once again slipping away. The trip had nearly exhausted the family and the funds. The town of Bisbee was booming in 1890 with the Purple Queen Mine and jobs were easy to come by. With Felix working the mine in Bisbee he could put food on the table for his growing family. The roof over their head continued to be a covered wagon.

"Sarah, children, come quickly I have news!" Felix was running and out of breath waving a paper wildly. "Sit down," he explained, "I received a telegram today." He began reading it out loud.

Papa has died. STOP. Sending your inheritance to bank in Bisbee. STOP.

Sarah gasped, "Oh children, you never knew your grandfather in Missouri but he was a good man, a godly man." Felix gathered the family together to offer a prayer of thanks for the life of Edward McEuen. As their eyes met after the prayer Felix and Sarah exchanged knowing looks. They would now have enough money to buy land and cattle. Lots of land and lots of cattle.

Felix's mind had not been idle while doing the back-breaking mine work. He had been asking and investigating where might be a good place for the family to begin ranching. He was particularly interested in the land along the Gila River. Water was the most precious commodity and the Gila, unlike many rivers or streams in Arizona, ran year round. He wanted much more land than the 160 acres the Homestead Act provided. There was much land available in the Gila River Valley and with the inheritance Felix purchased a whopping 130 sections of land from Wiley Holiday, around 200,000 acres! Felix and Sarah moved all 6 children to the new ranch. All that was there was a small cabin. Still,

Pearl's brothers. Photo courtesy of the Cromer family.

Pearl with her sister Lottie and friend Ida Woods, circa 1900. Courtesy of the Cromer family.

it was larger than the covered wagon and it was good to have a "home". Felix went to work with his herd, but his number one priority was to get his family into a real ranch house adequate for 9 people. His family was growing in number and in size with the boys all eventually growing to over 6' in height and strongly built. Sarah's first priority at the new cabin was to give birth to another son, Aron Felix. Sadly, Aron died at 6 months of age.

Pearl and Lottie stood in the middle of their very own bedroom with a real wood floor, a real roof and a nice window that looked out to the great expanse of the Gila River Valley. "Oh Lottie, it is so beautiful, I can't believe it!" exclaimed Pearl. "I know," added Lottie, "Now we have a kitchen, sitting room, a front door and six bedrooms." The family was the proud owner of the first wringer washing machine in the Gila River Valley. It sure beat the washboard! All the rooms were lined in redwood.

Sleep was difficult for the girls those first few weeks in the new house. Pearl and Lottie snuggled in one bed but

they missed their father's snoring and their mother's gentle caresses of a nursing infant. They even missed the "noise" of their brothers, now muted through the bedroom walls.

"Lottie! Come down and help with breakfast. Pearl, get Hazel dressed please." It was the first day of school and the McEuen family was ready for the wagon to take them to school four miles away in Ft. Thomas. The girls loved school. The boys could hardly wait to get back to the ranch. The girls did prefer riding their horses to the domestic chores that befell them. With the births of Hazel, Archie and Port, the family was now up to nine happy, healthy children. Each child had their own horse. Pearl's horse had a side saddle which all girls of that era used for riding. "Pearl, let me borrow your saddle," her older brother Marion begged. That was the problem with her saddle. Her brothers always wanted to borrow it. This was the ploy they used to court all the potential young women in the valley. Going riding with the McEuen boys was something all the young ladies in Safford and Thatcher were hoping for!

The family often enjoyed picnics at Indian Hot Springs. The springs were about a mile from home and the boys would ride their horses while the girls usually rode in the wagon with all the food for the picnic. The springs were surrounded by massive Cottonwood trees. With the summer temperatures often 105 or higher the springs were a welcome respite from the heat.

Another activity the boys participated in was boxing matches with each other. Setting up a ring in the front yard they expended lots of energy in this activity. The McEuen boys were known far and wide as rough and tough, and when you messed with one of them you messed with all of them. They

Archie McEuen, boxer on left getting ready to box at a match in southern Arizona, circa1920's. Courtesy of the Cromer family.

all were expert ropers, winning competitions as far away as Douglas.

"Pearl, you are the prettiest girl in town." Pearl read the note and laughed. People seemed to say it often enough, was it true? One of

A.F. McEuen family,
Courtesy of the Cromer/McEuen families

the young ranch hands certainly seemed to think so. Frank Cromer began courting Pearl and at the age of 22 she married him. Frank and Pearl continued to live on the ranch in Ft. Thomas.

"I can't believe it's a boy!" Pearl said to her doctor. I was sure it was going to be a girl, I was going to name her Thelma. I have always loved that name." "Well," her doctor laughed, "You can't name a boy Thelma!" He patted her arm and said, "He's a fine baby Pearl. Big and strong, you did well. I have a few things to do so I'll give you some time before I have to put a name on that birth certificate." Pearl was grateful for such a kind doctor. He was a wonderful man.

She thought desperately for a name. All the good names had been taken by her brothers or their sons. She didn't dare name the baby after one of them, that would cause a family feud for sure. Felix would be a good middle name. Her Doctor returned with a twinkle in his eye. "Any luck Pearl?" Pearl answered, "No, Dr. Sturgeon." Sturgeon. That was a nice, strong name. Suddenly Pearl smiled, "Dr. Sturgeon, I am going to name him after you. His name is Sturgeon Felix Cromer." Three years later Pearl got her daughter- Thelma, and then later another, Zola.

Sturgeon at age seven would ride his horse to school. His

grandmother Sarah, helping Pearl with the new baby, Zola told him, "Sturgeon, the Gila River is at flood stage, you be sure to use the bridge." Because he was seven and a boy, Sturgeon headed straight for the river. As he began to cross the river, his horse got tangled in barb wire. Miraculously, both horse and rider were able to escape the swollen river. Badly cut and bleeding Sturgeon rode his horse back home. His grandmother Sarah had little sympathy for the boy, doctored his cuts, changed his clothes and sent him back to the horse with these words, "Sturgeon, get to school, and this time use the bridge."

> "There are two kinds of people in Arizona: those who grew up in mining towns and those who wished they did." -Sam Borazon

After the birth of Zola, Frank took a job in the bustling town of Globe. He became Deputy Sheriff by day and ran card games at night in one of the rowdier saloons.

Pearl's children were growing up, but her marriage was in trouble. Frank found he was not fond of responsibility and took to a life of reckless living. After a short time he abandoned the family altogether and moved to California. Pearl found herself alone with three children, Sturgeon 11, Thelma 8 and Zola 4. The wealth of the McEuen ranch was not hers. It belonged to the brothers as land passed to the sons. Each one received 1/7 of the massive ranch to have as their own. Daughters were expected to find a husband.

Pearl moved the children to a tiny house, some called it a shack, on Yuma Street in Globe. The entire house was less than 500 square feet. The backyard hung onto a cliff that descended down to one of the many gulches running through Globe. One small pomegranate tree was all the front yard could hold. Pearl went to work for her sister, Hazel, who was running a boarding house for miners. With Sturgeon and Thelma in school she took little Zola along with her while she cleaned, cooked and did laundry for the miners. Sturgeon excelled in school, lettering in a number of sports. Thelma also was an excellent athlete running races in which the miners would frequently bet on her to win. Zola brimmed with character and bright red hair, also excelling in school. Sturgeon wanted to become a teacher, but there wasn't any money for further education. He spent two years working in the Old Dominion Mine in Globe until he had saved enough for his first year of college. He wanted to go to Flagstaff to the Arizona State Teachers College. After he completed his first year of school he returned home for the summer hoping again to work in the Old Dominion Mine for money for the fall semester. It was 1929 and the Depression was taking a toll on families across the nation, including Globe. He approached the mine foreman who said to him, "Sturgeon, see these men lined up looking for work? They got wives and family. I'm gonna hire you cause you are trying to better yourself and your helping your Ma. But when you come to work, go in the back door."

Upon graduation from college, Sturgeon returned to Globe where he taught high school and coached several sports. One memorable day at a football game he looked out on the field to see a descendent of the Tewksbury family, the running back, and a descendent of the Graham family, the quarterback, chatting happily with one another. Sturgeon smiled and wondered if they understood the significance of it all.

After all her children had graduated from high school Pearl took an "easier" job at the high school cafeteria. Every morning she got up at 3 a.m. and walked the three miles to school. She put in a full day there, and walked back three miles home. She held this job for over 30 years, working well into her 80's. Although the cafeteria work was hard, espe-

Pearl, first on left, with the other ladies who cooked in the cafeteria at Globe High School, circa 1950's. Courtesy of the Cromer/McEuen families.

47

cially being on her feet all day, Pearl made many friends and enjoyed all the students. She knew them by name and knew their parents, brothers and sisters, aunts and uncles. When she wasn't at work she could be found at church. Raised as a Methodist, she settled in at the Church of Christ in Globe. Serving in many capacities she was a blessing to everyone who knew her. "She was a wonderful, kind woman," said her grandson, Mike Cromer. His wife Sarah added, "Everyone in the extended family said she never had a bad thing to say about anyone and no one ever said a bad thing about her."

Pearl's father, Felix died at age 84. Her mother, at age 66 was devastated at the loss. Another loss three years later was her son Amos who died at 44. Sarah was faced with a huge challenge when her son Archie's wife died. They had two sons. Sarah took care of Willis who was only 6 years old. To take on the responsibility of a rambunctious six year old boy at age 69 is indeed a daunting task. Hazel raised Willis' brother, Ross. When Willis was 15 and Sarah was nearing 80, they came to live in Pearl's tiny house on Yuma street. It was a happy time for Sarah and Willis. Willis recalls that Pearl would meet him at the front door and dance with him across the tiny living room into the kitchen. No matter what events impacted her life, she was always happy.

Even though her house was tiny she had an open door policy for anyone who needed food or lodging. Everyone loved to stay with "Aunt Pearl". Globe was the "big city" in south eastern Arizona and many people came and went for doctor visits, legal matters and shopping. She cared for her mother Sarah, as she advanced in age and Sarah wrote to a friend, "Pearl cares for me like I was a baby."

In 1934, Sturgeon married his college sweetheart, Dorothy Hines and they settled down in Globe. Dorothy gave birth to their only child, Michael in 1941. Sturgeon eventually became Superintendent of the Flagstaff Public Schools and held the position for 24 years. He was as kind and caring as his mother had been. He once took chicken soup and a six pack of coke to a teacher who had fallen ill. On another occasion he arranged housing and a roommate for a new teacher and actually picked her up at the train. Cromer Elementary in Flagstaff was named for him. In 1971 he was named Flagstaff Citizen of the Year.

Thelma married a mine superintendent and lived in or near Globe most of her life, spending lots of time with her mother.

Zola moved frequently and traveled extensively, but came back to Globe towards the end of her life and took care of her mother.

Pearl had three grandchildren. Sturgeon had a son, Michael. Thelma had a son, Don. Zola had a daughter, Elaine.

Pearl remained close with her brothers and sisters. Her brothers continued ranching into their 70's and 80's with no thought of retiring. The Sanders family who had traveled to the Arizona Territory with the McEuens also became successful cattle ranchers. They established herds near Globe and also in Pleasant Valley. The Sanders Family reunion continues to this day, and is held every year in Pleasant Valley. Lottie moved to California so Pearl did not see her often, but Hazel remained in the Globe-Miami area.

Pearl was active into her mid-nineties. At age 95 she suffered a stroke from which she never fully recovered. She died in 1982 at the age of 98.

Life facts:
Frank Cromer birth and death unknown
Pearl 1884-1982
Sturgeon 1908-1992
Thelma 1911-1980
Zola 1914-2010

Grandchildren 3

Favorite quote: "I'm so glad to see you."

Favorite recipe: Jerky Gravy with Biscuits

The Mis-Adventures: Credit where credit is due-to the inept, the unsober and the uncoordinated, October 1971

Verner G. Benson

Everyone believes gold mines are discovered by hardy, adventurous men wise in the ways of veins, shafts, slopes and drifts. Don't believe it. Most mines were discovered by the inept, the unsober and the uncoordinated.

Although the Globe area is now noted for its copper deposits, it was first settled in 1876 following a silver strike. The boom was caused by the discovery of a globe – shaped boulder of almost pure silver, with markings not unlike those on a world globe.

As I understand it the gentleman who discovered it fell over it first, ruined a toe on one foot, got mad, let fly at the boulder with the other foot, found this to be impractical and sat down. While nursing his feet he noticed that the boulder had not moved. A scratch with his knife showed the true composition and the feet were forgotten. It was quite a boom while it lasted, with everyone in the territory rushing into the Apache hunting ground where the boulder was found, falling over boulders and kicking the smaller rocks. The Apaches were not happy with their new neighbors and called the tent village Besh-Ba-Gowah, the metal village. That seems awfully mild for the Apaches, so their comments may have been censored.

The discovery of copper four years later was the last straw for the Apaches and they made things warm for the miners until the surrender of Geronimo in 1886.

The discovery of the Crown King mine was a classic example of the unsober combining forces with the unskilled. In 1876 an Army officer, wishing to keep valid a mining claim, hired a prospector to perform the necessary work. The officer returned to Fort Whipple and the prospector, meeting jovial and thirsty friends at Old Tiger Camp, deputized two bullwhackers to do the assessment work.

Lacking badges, he conferred his official sanction with long pulls from his jug. While the bullwhackers were willing, they lacked experience with drill and hammer. Striking rock within a few inches of the surface they and the jug decided to look for softer ground. Within moments a vein about four inches wide and reasonably soft was opened and the bullwhackers happily went after it. Visiting a neighboring camp that evening they told of the odd soft material, telling it was brass or iron pirates or something, and produced a piece of it. It was the first of many gold strikes in the area.

A somewhat uncoordinated gentleman known as "Shorty" Alger was grubstaked by Dick Wick Hall. Prospecting in the Harcuvar Mountains, Shorty was climbing a small, steep hill north of Tank Pass when he slipped. To save himself from falling again, Shorty stuck his pick in the ground. When the pick was pulled out a small nugget was found impaled on the point. From this "glory hole" more than $100,000 in gold was taken. Uncoordination had paid off again.

Near McMillanville, now a ghost town, silver was discovered by the uninitiated. Charles McMillan and Dory Harris, a tenderfoot, joined forces on a prospecting trip. All went well until McMillan went on a spree in town. Preparing for the morning after, McMillan brought back not only the hair of the dog that bit him but the dog as well. Morning found him gloriously and beautifully drunk.

Time, however, finally took its toll. McMillan laid down on some soft stones for a nap. Harris, while waiting for McMillan to be released from the arms of Morpheus and Bacchus, idly chopped at a moss – covered ledge nearby. A chunk broke off and Harris noticed it seemed to be webbed with a dull metallic substance. Harris stuck it in his pocket to show it to McMillan later. McMillan woke and seemed to be somewhat grumpy so it was some time before Harris dared show him the rock. It contained a high percentage of native silver and the Stonewall Jackson Mine brought riches to both men.

One of the most casual finds occurred in 1863. An expedition led by A. H. Peeples entered Arizona at Yuma, picked up famous scout Pauline Weaver and strolled to La Paz. The Mexicans panning gold in La Paz did not seem overly friendly and the party crossed the mountains and entered the Cullen Valley. While Weaver pursued antelope the rest of the party panned gold in a nearby stream. Four Mexicans who had joined the party at Yuma set out to look for their strayed horses. They returned that evening and showed Peeples a number of gold nuggets they had found on the top of a nearby mountain.

The next morning the four Mexicans loaded their gold into saddle bags and rode back into Mexico, chattering happily. The rest of the party rode to the top of the mountain, chattering excitedly. In a sloping basin lay the nuggets. It is said that Peeples picked up $7,000 worth of gold before breakfast. I am quite willing to believe the $7,000 but am unwilling to believe that he stopped for breakfast. The place was Rich Hill near Congress Junction. It is estimated that during the first month a quarter of a million dollars in gold was found.

Henry Wickenburg's burro is said to have been directly responsible for the greatest gold discovery in Arizona. The burro strayed and Wickenburg pursued. In the manner of men since time began Wickenburg spoke softly to the burro, flattered him, promised him delicacies and then cursed him, first softly and then with vehemence. Failing in this, he chucked rocks at him. The rocks fell short, being exceptionally heavy. Wickenburg soon discovered the weight was caused by a large percentage of gold. In this manner was the Vulture mine discovered.

In these ways may be discovered all the famous, fabulously rich lost mines. Lost mines, like lost fish, are always fabulous. Someone will fall in them or over them. A map drawn on a bit of parchment is a great help but so, apparently, are two left feet.

Globe's First Christmas: Celebration in a Saloon

Reprinted from the Gila Centennial book, "Honor the Past, Mold the Future."
Courtesy of Gila County Museum.

It was December 1876. Word had gone out to the prospectors in the hills and the people in the camp that Knox and McNelly would have a Christmas tree in their saloon, with everyone invited, and that the bar and gambling room would be closed during the event.

They approved heartily, and vowed to make the celebration an honored success. For, with all their wild, boisterous and rough-hewn exterior, there was a sentimental streak in all of them. To the hardy and indomitable pioneers of Globe the thought of Christmas Eve brought the same ageless memories of home and childhood that is associated with it in the hearts of millions all over the world.

The Knox and McNelly Saloon was one of the finest in the southwest. Its bar was of bronze oak and its mahogany surface shone like glass. The back bar, too, was highly ornate, with a long mirror, adorned with glass chandeliers, beautiful vases, goblets and drinking vessels.

Huge Rochester oil lamps, suspended by other glass chandeliers, illuminated the large spacious hall. Gambling layouts, faro, roulette, monte and poker games were played in the back part and the respective tables were crowded every day and night, thousands of dollars being won and lost daily.

Celebrating the birth of Christ in a saloon -however elegant- was the talk of the whole territory at the time. Committees had been appointed to select presents for the pioneer families. A beautiful pine tree was brought from the Pinal Mountains and set up in the saloon, filling the house with an unaccustomed fragrance. Eight inches at the base, ten feet high with tapering branches one to four feet in length, it was undoubtedly a tree fit for such a historic occasion. Red, white, yellow, green, blue and brown ribbons were draped and twined around its boughs and trunk. Candles were arranged to shed their soft and flickering glow, and the presents were placed under the resplendent boughs.

The saloon had been closed during the preparations, and its bar, back bar and gambling tables were covered with white muslin cloth, as one of the gamblers said, "To clear the minds of the most pious and to prove to the skeptical that the celebration was in spirit and in truth a real Christian affair.

It had been gently snowing through the day and when night came the little camp was wrapped in a mantle of white. The rutted road through camp and rough board sidewalks shone brilliantly where the light from shacks and buildings along the way illuminated patches of frozen snow. At eight o'clock the doors were opened and *people came drifting in. There was an usher to direct them to places where they were to stand and an officer who quietly asked, "Did you leave your gun at home?" "Yep," "Sure," and "You bet your life," were the usual replies. One brawny miner noted for his quick trigger finger growled his reply with the added comment, "Any man that would start a rumpus on a night like this orter be strung up on a sycamore."*

It was a typical western crowd that waited the coming of the pioneer women and their children, who were the honored guests; stalwart, broad-chested, bearded men from the mines and trails, wearing hobnail or cowhide boots, blue jeans, red, blue or brown shirts, low-crowned hats and mackinaws or blanket lined ducking and buckskin coats. The town folk wore "store clothes", while the gamblers wore the most immaculate suits, boots and shoes, hats and derbies. They addressed one another in subdued tones. There was no levity or suggestion of ridicule, but rather a feeling of pressed emotion as they waited.

Finally they came, the women and children of Globe's earliest days. Dressed carefully in their plain, neat clothes, coarse shoes, and scarfs or shawls over their heads, they rather timidly approached the lighted tree. Bill McNelly, master of ceremonies made welcoming remarks and Felix Knox-dead game hunter, gambler and gentleman-assured them the wonderful Christmas tree was for their pleasure and everyone would be disappointed if they did not enjoy it.

The reserve was broken and one lady spoke, "Mr. McNelly, I wonder if we cannot have a few words of prayer from someone?" This was a stickler for McNelly, he had over-looked a bet. But without hesitation he replied, "Sure, Ma'am." Then he called out, "Is there anyone here who has real honest religion enough in his toughened soul to give us a word of prayer?"

Out of the crowd stepped a tall, powerful man with black beard, blue eyes and black hair hanging almost to his shoulders, blue shirt opened at the throat, brown jeans tucked in cowhide boots.

He took his stance at the side of the Christmas tree and began to speak in a clear mellow voice. He told of the scene in Bethlehem centuries ago, when Christ was born: He recounted the sufferings of the Savior and His death and resurrection. His hearers stood spellbound. Handkerchiefs were seen wiping away starting tears upon women's cheeks, and men drew further back into the crowd to hide their emotions as he quoted a verse.

In the profound stillness that followed, this stranger walked to the doorway and disappeared into the night. No one tried to stop him; no one knew who he was. It was several minutes before the spell was broken and the distribution of gifts got under way. At last the rejoicing and merriment waned, and children began to tire and the families went off to their homes through the sparkling snow. The men who remained milled around a little awkwardly for a while, but the urge to be themselves at all costs was too strong: the bar and tables were stripped of their chaste coverings and opened for business. Amid songs, happy greetings and general good cheer, the old carefree life of the frontier was in full swing again.

That then is the story of Globe's first Christmas tree, and as we compared old versions of the story, something of the spirit of that unique celebration came through, and we are inclined with one old-timer who wrote, "With all due respect to churches that are dedicated to celebrate this transcendent event, let it be said here that no gathering of people in cathedral hall or simple church ever paid a more reverent homage to the Maker of mankind than the rough hewn citizens of the mining camp of Globe that memorable Christmas Eve in 1876."

CHAPTER FIVE

Veronica
Michelbach
1877-1972

Young Veronica, circa 1895. Photo courtesy of Michelbach family collection

Story as told by her granddaughter Marilyn Michelbach Coy.

When the ship, Noordland embarked from Antwerp, Belgium, in 1892, it included Veronica Schwab sailing for America. On the German dominated manifest of passengers filling fourteen pages was listed Veronica and four of her friends all heading for New York. She was the youngest of her group at 15 years of age. A photo taken the year of her arrival reflects a serious young girl with a firmly set mouth. Was she a no nonsense kind of young woman, or perhaps insecure in her new surroundings and putting on a determined face for the camera?

She was leaving her home in Boxberg, Germany, her two half-brothers and two half-sisters. "Fronie" as she was called by the younger ones in the family was older by 7 years than her first half-sibling, a brother. According to an Arizona Daily Sun interview, her intentions were to work for five years in America and return home. But why was she leaving home so early? One wonders if family dynamics weren't part of the impetus for Veronica's leaving. Her half-sister, Maria Schwab

Sauer, would later relate that Veronica's birth father was a high-placed and well known German industrialist and businessman. Her mother brought little "Veronika" with her to her marriage to Schwab. Possibly Veronica wanted to experience a world outside Boxberg.

Veronica also left behind a young suitor named Peter Michelbach whom she had known throughout her childhood. Peter had fallen in love with Veronica and asked her to delay her departure until he was finished with his military service in the army of Kaiser Wilhelm II. She turned him down.

Peter and Veronica, before they were married. Photo courtesy of Charlene Benham.

She arrived in New York to begin working as a domestic and nanny for a family in New Jersey who sponsored her. She knew no English when she arrived and learned her new language from her surroundings. In later years she would humorously tell the story on herself when her employer asked her to please get him a hemd (which means shirt in German). She misunderstood and retrieved a ham, confusing the two familiar sounding German/English words. The

Homestead cabin built in 1897, Hart Prairie. Photo courtesy of Mary Lou Davis.

embarrassment was compounded by the fact that this German-Jewish family would not have been asking for "ham". She stayed in the East, probably with this family, for five more years

Peter Michelbach arrived in America two years after Veronica in January 1894 on the Trave. He located Veronica and they rekindled their friendship. He did not like the east and asked Veronica to marry him and move west. It is not known if she accepted or possibly delayed her answer because of her five year commitment.

Westward bound, Peter first stopped in Albuquerque where his older brother who had sponsored him lived, and he worked as a butcher in his brother's grocery store. By August he had joined his older sister, Barbara, who with her husband was homesteading at the nearly 8,300 feet elevation on Hart Prairie. Like the several German settlers who homesteaded in Hart Prairie, Peter loved the mountain, covered with pine, fir and groves of aspen. There was abundant wildlife. Peter filed for a homestead on acreage abutting his sister's. Hart Prairie must have reminded German settlers of their native country since so many old German names still abound in landmarks in that area.

Peter and Veronica kept a correspondence back and forth until she finally agreed to marry Peter. She did not return home to Germany but arrived in Flagstaff in 1897 and they were married in 1898 in the first Catholic Church of the Nativity on the south side of Flagstaff in Old Town on property once owned but donated by PJ Brannen. The build-

From L to R, Barbara, Peter, Joe, Eva, Veronica and Mary. Circa 1903. Photo courtesy of Mary Lou Davis.

ing would later become Brannen School.

By their first year Peter had finished a two-room house he built for the two of them at 723 West Aspen. Over the following years the house was expanded and remolded into a two-story 6+ bedroom home for their large family, 11 children in all. The couple lived there 66 years until Peter's death at age 93.

During their early years, Peter hauled logs for the lumber mill and he used his talents as a butcher working at the meat-packing house for Babbitt's.

Veronica and Peter's family of the eventual eight daughters and three sons began that next year with the birth of a baby girl, and she continued to have children for the next 21 years, having her last one at age 43. The children grew up literally vying and competing for "Mamma's" attention and affection.

Peter and Veronica began right away farming and ranching at the homestead in Hart Prairie. They planted oat hay that was sold to the Arizona Lumber and Timber Mill as feed for the draft horses. They also planted potatoes which won blue ribbons at county and state fairs. The children told stories of how their mother, always in a dress or skirt, worked tirelessly alongside Peter pitching hay from atop the hay stacks to feed the horse-drawn baler or helping with the planting in the fields. When not in the field she would stop to nurse a baby or prepare meals for the family and laborers. Remembrances of the children include how the older children were to watch over the baby in a wash tub in the field

Peter in the center, with his two sons, left, A.P. and on his right, Joe. Photo courtesy of Marilyn Michelbach Coy.

Fisher helps the children with the harvest. Left to Right: Fisher, Barbara, Minnie, Rose, AP, and Mary. Photo courtesy of Mary Lou Davis.

while Veronica was helping Peter. She would follow Peter as he plowed with a horse and single blade plow, dropping potatoes in the furrows, one by one or she would scatter oat hay seed by hand while Peter plowed. The Michelbach and neighboring homesteaders, including Peter's sister, Barbara Lohe England, the families of Dillman Friedenberger, Beech, Black, and Fischer helped with each other's harvest, each taking time to go to the others' homesteads.

Lives revolved around the changing seasons of Northern Arizona which also meant changing where one lived during what season. On their homestead in Hart Prairie, Peter built a one room log cabin for the new family. Through the years additions were made. Part of the original cabin still stands today on the homestead. By the late 1930's a new farm house was constructed and stood until it was destroyed by fire in 1994.

Spring meant getting in the crops at the ranch, but before Veronica left her house in town, she traditionally planted sweet peas on St. Patrick's Day outside the dining room window. On the east side of the house in town stood her huge garden where she planted cabbage, corn, lettuce, turnips, strawberries, rhubarb, carrots, radishes, and onions, but it was her cabbage that was most noted since it was to be used in her legendary sauerkraut. As one walked in the door, the aroma of fermenting sauerkraut is a memory of all her grandchildren. A crock sat in the pantry, the cellar or a corner of the kitchen depending on time of year and temperature in the house.

The other aroma that family members happily conjure up was the smell of her delicious signature cinnamon rolls. Saturdays were traditionally the day she baked the rolls, bread, pie and coffee kuchen. A granddaughter remembers that the first dozen cinnamon rolls out of the oven were taken to the

1938, Grandson, Albert, floating in a pond formed by Hart Prairie Spring. Photo courtesy of Marilyn Michelbach Coy.

parish house. The little granddaughter would deliver them, knowing that Veronica had packed one extra for her granddaughter to enjoy with the parish housekeeper.

The "house in town" on Aspen Avenue also included a barn area behind the house. That is where Peter kept his draft horses for the wagon and sleigh, ranch horses, ducks, chickens, rabbits, milk cow and at times big white hogs to be slaughtered. When Peter slaughtered the pig, he would hang it upside down, cut the throat and while the blood ran out, Veronica would be below, whipping the blood that would be used for Blutwurst to be mixed with other ingredients to make sausage and head cheese (a cold cut using the meat from the hog's head). All parts of the animal were used. Veronica would clean the casings (intestines) of the hog so that they could be used later for Peter's famous sausage. The other part of the hog was used as pork or ham. Any surplus food, milk from the cow, or vegetables was given to the nuns and the parish house.

Canning was done with seasonal fruits, stored in the cellar, along with Veronica's tasty homemade root beer. Peter stored his homemade beer and elderberry wine there as well. Potatoes were kept there for next year's planting. Peter built for Veronica a huge kitchen even in today's terms. The family enjoyed a sunny eat-in kitchen area, large dining room, spacious parlor/living room with beveled glass French doors dividing the rooms. A beautiful slate fireplace was at one end of the parlor and on the carpet were Navajo rugs. One wonders if those rugs might have been given to the family as Veronica told stories of when Navajos would quietly slip into the house. She would turn around and there they were in her kitchen. Usually they were there requesting food, which she generously gave. Maybe a rug or two came from a "thank you" for her kindness?

As spring approached, the family would move to the ranch. Peter would load "Mamma", the kids and her sewing machine in the wagon for the 14 mile trip along dirt and sometimes heavily rutted roads to the homestead. The children were taken out of parochial school and attended the one-room mountain school for those few weeks left in the school year. The children would drive the wagon or ride their horses the 2-4 miles to the school. The school was probably the historic Summit School located on the old Hochderffer property. One of the children "young Pete" (AP) told

Veronica, 1948. Photo courtesy Dorotha Mae Moore.

the story that he was too young to attend school but yearned to go. One day he hid in the buckboard so he could go with his older siblings. Veronica was frantic when she could not find him. Young Pete was duly punished by Papa for having given Veronica such a fright. The school house was also used for summer dances where neighbors and ranchers could get together. Veronica said she sat out the dances because Peter was providing the music for others. Peter, being a talented musician, played his concertina. He had performed with it at Heidelberg Castle when still in Germany, an honor he told about throughout his lifetime.

At the ranch, they kept their food cool by placing a wet burlap bag over it. Water was provided by a spring about 1/4 of a mile from the farm house. At one time the spring was so productive that a pond was big enough for the kids to float a small homemade raft on it. Water was carried to the house from the spring using a human "yoke" with two buckets on either side to balance the weight of the water. Veronica and the children would pick gooseberries throughout the spring and summer—green and hard ones for her gooseberry jelly, and the later ripened ones for her pies, or those "just for eating". She was an expert mushroom hunter or so she thought until one time when she picked some that made her gravely ill. From then on she stopped picking mushrooms that grew in the aspen groves. Whether at the ranch or in town, Veronica was a fastidious house keeper. Veronica made her own soap, washed clothes on a washboard, heated water in a copper kettle on the wood stove from wood chopped by the boys. Her "sensible" quilts were made from sturdy fabric for the cold mountain nights, but she also quilted some lovely ones for "in town". Fresh butter, cream and cottage cheese were staples. The "Quark" (German for clabber, cheese/sour cream) was taken over the hill to the homestead of Peter's sister, Tante (aunt) Barbara to enjoy since she was the only one in the family who liked it. Spring was a time for branding, with neighboring ranchers helping out on round-up. Fall meant moving the cattle to the winter ranch north of Flagstaff, near Cameron. The family owned the Lazy PM brand throughout territorial days then added the Quarter Circle Cross X brand in 1915. The brand is still being used today.

Veronica and Peter, 1958. Photo courtesy of Dorotha Mae Moore.

Veronica was a devout Catholic. One wonders if her serious religious side was not a result of some compensation from her early childhood. Veronica always kept a rosary in her apron pocket. She was known to assemble a small May Day altar that included flowers and candles in one of the rooms near her bedroom. She walked to church daily, even into old age. Sally Zanzucchi tells of Veronica in later years sometimes stopping by her house after daily mass to just visit while Sally did her ironing. Sally recalls that Veronica was always a happy and cheerful visitor.

Like many of the early parishioners, the Michelbach family had a reserved pew at Nativity church with a family name plate. The family helped with the building of the church by donating lichen-covered malapai rock transported in the wagon from the ranch. Peter estimated that he hauled over 200 wagon loads. The church on Cherry Avenue was completed in 1930 after several years in construction. Easter, Christmas and Thanksgiving were huge gatherings of family and neighbors. Christmas memories include the large crèche Veronica placed in the front window of the house in town and when she and Peter would sing O'Tannenbaum in their native tongue of German by their Christmas tree before the family dispersed to Midnight Mass.

Veronica had some well known remedies that she passed down: Epsom salts with turpentine to soak one's foot for a rusty nail; putting vinegar on a bee or wasp sting; cough medicine made from syrup of onions and sugar slowly heated over a stove; mustard plasters

1925 Family Photo. Standing: Barbara, Joe, Eva, AP, Rose, Cecilia, Minnie Seated: Mary, Veronica, Frank, Peter and Theresa. Photo courtesy Charlene Benham.

for colds, blackberry brandy or castor oil. Her daughter-in-law, Ann Michelbach, attributed a remedy Veronica administered to their young baby, Albert, to break his fever to recover from scarlet fever.

Unfortunately one life she couldn't save was their baby daughter, Agnes in 1918. 18 month-old Agnes died as a result of the Spanish Flu brought by the World War I troops on trains stopping in town. Daughter, Mary, told that the flu swept through town and their family as it did worldwide.

The Spanish Flu

Spain took a bad rap getting tagged with the worst epidemic ever to hit mankind. During WW1, neutral Spain was the only country that was reporting this new and serious flu virus, hence Spanish Flu. It started in the spring of 1918, hardly noticeable with a few deaths here and there. By August of 1918 a terror was sweeping the world. A healthy robust young man or women in their early 20's could have a sniffle in the morning and be dead that night. Unlike other illness a healthy immune system was your worst enemy. It caused the immune system to have an extreme response that attacked the body, destroying organs in hours. Lungs filled with blood and looked more like a liver. People turned very dark and it was impossible to recognize race. 40-100 million people died around the world, the true number will never be known. It hit young people so hard that the average life expectancy dropped that year to 39. It also took a terrible toll on pregnant women and Native peoples. Whole native communities were wiped out. The Iditarod sled dog race in Alaska is a reenactment of a real race to try to get medicine and supplies to the outlying Eskimo villages. It almost single handily ended WW1, the men on all sides were simply too ill to fight. America lost 6,000 soldiers in one week! It killed more people than WW1, WW2, the Korean War and the Vietnam War all put together. It peaked in October and November and by the end of 1919 had virtually disappeared. People over 40 seemed to be immune, probably from a previous flu that ravaged the world in 1882-83.

She remembered that the old Emerson School was used for beds for the flu-stricken residents in Flagstaff.

10 of the 11 Michelbach children lived to adulthood. The children were all expected to work without complaint at home and the farm/ranch. AP (young Pete) said, "Damn that old man made us work!"

Peter was a task master and the children all said he was a difficult man with an unbending mean streak--but never to Veronica. Throughout their lives there was a need by Peter and her children to win and hold her affection. She seemed to dismiss or ignore contentious and unpleasant situations in the family. Yet her children forgave her for that and talked about her being gentle, warm, pious and loving...a compensation, to be sure, to Peter's behavior.

One obligation in the family was to attend Sunday mass, no exceptions. In the early years, the young family walked to mass to the church in Old Town south of the tracks. The family would start out an hour early to make services and for the boys to serve as altar boys. The children loved to dash across the railroad tracks to and from church and once one of the sisters lost her new hat for Easter down the tracks. Heartbroken, she wanted to go after it, but was not allowed, no tears and church awaited!

Delivering groceries in the snow to Lowell Observatory, 1948. Courtesy of Marilyn Michelbach Coy.

Cold and severe winters were known in Flagstaff in the old days. Because Peter had a horse-drawn sleigh, he would deliver groceries to the snowbound residents. Well into his 80's he was still voluntarily shoveling out neighbors' driveways and walks. He never learned to drive a car and older Flagstaff residents remember as kids, hitching a ride on his wagon drawn by two horses as he drove through town on Ft. Valley Road going home.

People remember Veronica's vivid blue eyes, soft skin and her long white hair worn in a bun. She never wore makeup but never seemed to age. She was known by residents as a person whose generosity spilled over to neighbors or neighbors' children, especially if she felt they needed a good home-cooked meal. She took under her wing one close-by family for many years. The men from that family called her "grandma" all their lives. Her own children referred to her as an angel or a saint, probably as a result of life-long dealing with Peter.

She spoke German when she and Peter "exchanged words" or when scolding "Papa" when Peter would get too long-winded in his storytelling!

Veronica lived to 95 years of age and saw most of her 19 grandchildren grow to adulthood.

In 1963, Veronica and Peter were nominated as The Arizona Daily Sun's "Northland Couple of the Year" by John and Betty Babbitt, E. C. and Bess Slipher, Russell and Mary Sweitzer, and C. Otto and Louise Black. The quote from the paper reads, "On February 14th, Arizona will have celebrated 51 years of statehood and with this in mind, we wish to place before you, not the man or woman of the year but the couple of the year"....a wonderful tribute to two remarkable Flagstaff pioneer settlers.

Life Facts:
11 children:

Eva Elizabeth	1899-1983
Joseph Thomas	1900-1945
Barbara Marie	1902-1998
Mary Kathryn	1903-1991
Albert Peter	1905-1998
Theresa Veronica	1907-1986
Cecilia Odelia	1909-1993
Minnie (Philomena)	1912-2007
Margarita Rosa	1913-1979
Agnes Mary	1916-1918
Francis Lawrence	1920-1997

Grandchildren: 19

Favorite recipes: cinnamon rolls, sauerkraut

Veronica's story is from information gathered by granddaughter, Marilyn Michelbach Coy, from Arizona Daily Sun newspaper articles about Peter and Veronica, ancestry documentation research, a personal journal of Veronica's daughter, Barbara, provided by Mary Lou Davis, phone conversations with Theresa's daughter, Dorotha Mae Moore, phone conversations from Mary's daughter, Charlene Benham, the transcribed 1976 interview of daughters, Eva and Mary located at the NAU library, conversations with grandniece, Pat Hill and reminiscences by the author's siblings, Dorothy Weinberg and Dr. Albert Michelbach, MD.

Cutting hay on Hart Prairie, 1952. Photo by George McCullough. Photo courtesy of Marilyn Michelbach Coy.

Peg Leg

Verner G. Benson

Author's note: My Dad wrote this story in 1972. It was the only serious story he ever wrote. He was a very sensitive man and I think it was hard for him to write this. It was certainly hard for me to read it, I cry every time. I probably would not have ever included it in my books except that it fits so perfectly with the story of Veronica. The Michelbachs were friends with the ranchers and others mentioned in the story and of course were very well aware of Peg Leg.

Flagstaff, Arizona, just after the turn of the century, was a small logging and cattle town, consisting mostly of saloons, a store or two and a lumber mill. North of Flagstaff lie the SanFrancisco Peaks, highest in Arizona, called the "Peaks" or more often simply the "Mountain." Beginng in the summer of 1909 the entire area was terrorized by a one-legged man wearing a hand-made wooden leg.

The Peaks are high, covered with growths of aspen, fir and pine to timberline, cut with steep canyons, and dotted with boulders the size of railroad locomotives. In the early 1900's several small hay ranches nestled on the lower slopes. They and a few line shacks, used during the summer months by cow outfits, were the only habitations.

Terrifying is an odd way to describe Peg Leg, as he was called, because he hurt no one, accosted no one: in fact, there is no record of his even speaking to anyone. Occasionally he broke into isolated ranch homes and took food and ammunition but never more than he needed. Valuables were left untouched. The terror, and it was very real, came from the mystery of the man himself. He avoided people, he was seen but unknown, ---and the unknown, especially in isolated places is always frightening.

He wandered all over the mountain, scrambling up slopes difficult for a man with two good legs to climb, yet was seen only at a distance. On rare occasions he was spotted clumping along the trails which passed for roads in that area but before the wagon or rider could catch up with him he had darted off into the underbrush and disappeared. Late at night a fire, thought to be Peg Leg's, could be seen high on the mountain, but no matter how quickly investigators might arrive the fire would be out, the ashes scattered, and Peg Leg gone.

Women at isolated cabins locked their doors, an unusual thing in itself, and refused to venture out after dark. Lonely herders kept one eye on their flocks and the other eye out for Peg Leg. Children were frightened by the very mention of his name.

Descriptions of Peg Leg are vague, at best. He apparently was of medium height, medium age and medium coloring. And he always carried a huge pack on his back.

Dutch Dillman, a treasured friend of mine, was living on the north slope of the Peaks during the years when Peg Leg roamed. Dutch well remembered seeing Peg Leg pass their ranch for the last time in the summer of 1912. Dutch's description of Peg Leg's appearance is as vague as the others, yet Dutch has spent years in the woods and ordinarily could see a turkey or a deer where no one else could.

However, he can remember the imprint of Peg Leg's wooden leg perfectly and describes it as round and smooth in the soft dirt of the road. His memory dispels the widespread rumor that Peg Leg wore an old shoe turned backward to baffle pursuit. This rumor was of course, nonsense. Even the most unskilled of trackers could have told at once by the scuffed dirt, the broken weeds or dislodged pebbles which way Peg Leg was going. Dean Eldridge of Flagstaff had on display in his museum a wooden leg claimed to be Peg Leg's. Attached to the shaft was a shoe, old shrunken and distorted in the manner of all old shoes. Others claim Peg Leg's wooden leg was laid to rest with him.

On the afternoon Dutch saw Peg Leg pass the Dillman ranch he watched him continue up the mountain to a ranch known as the Hart place, and saw him make camp close by. Shortly afterward a chuck wagon with some cowboys in attendance passed the Dillman ranch headed in the direction of the Hart place. Peg Leg, on seeing the wagon's approach, hurriedly stuffed his gear into his pack and disappeared.

The next morning the cowboys, now accompanied by a county ranger, Ed Johnson, traveled farther up the mountain to what was then known as the "Wild Bill" cabin. As they approached, Peg Leg ran out of the only door to the cabin. Johnson jumped from his horse and, ordering Peg leg to throw up his hands, moved forward. Instead of complying with Johnson's order Peg Leg reached under his shirt as though to grab a gun. The ranger fired, his bullet striking Peg Leg in the forehead, between the eyes, and killing him instantly. Peg Leg died as he lived, silently.

Peg Leg did have a gun beneath his shirt. It was an old, inexpensive, nickel-plated revolver and there are those that say it would not have harmed a cat unless one threw it at him. The body was left where it had fallen and a rider was dispatched to fetch the sheriff. When the sheriff arrived the body was thoroughly searched. Nothing could be found that bore Peg Leg's name or any clue to his identity. The pack contained only food, a few pieces of clothing, battered cooking utensils, and a sawed-off shotgun.

Peg Leg was taken to Flagstaff and for three days the body lay in a local hardware store in the hope that it might be identified. Nothing. There were rumors that a stranger, bearing a resemblance to Peg Leg came to the store's window several times and looked at him sadly. If it is true, he never entered the place.

The death of Peg Leg seemed only to deepen the mystery. Why had he attempted to draw a gun on the ranger? Was Peg Leg deaf and dumb—unable to understand the ranger's command? Had he been attempting to merely surrender the gun? Or was Peg Leg mentally unbalanced? The thought must have crossed the ranger's mind and caused him many a sleepless night. Law officers might be required to shoot people at times but they are not required to enjoy it.

Looking back, Peg Leg's death seems so unnecessary. The most serious charge which could have been brought against him was petty theft. Had he waved or stopped to jaw a little with the people living around the Peaks they would have feared him not at all. He might have been "wanted" elsewhere but so were many people in Arizona. No one could blame Johnson; it was a period when a man reached for a gun, it was unlikely he intended to polish it. Peg Leg was buried in the old Flagstaff Cemetery, but later moved and his gravesite is lost. Peg Leg's silence remains unbroken. Maybe he wanted it *that way. Dying, for him, might have been easier than living with his fellow men. I have always wished though, every time I've heard the story, that the lonely man could have been buried on his mountain. He must have loved it a very great deal.*

CHAPTER SIX

𝓡uth Jordan

1902-1996

*Ruth Jordan, photo
courtesy of Sedona
Heritage Museum
(Sedona, AZ).*

"𝓗is name is Pet," David told Ruth Woolf. "He is so gentle," added David's sister Virginia. As the three friends walked across the field toward the barn Ruth was grateful for all the encouragement she could get. A mere 5 foot tall and at best 90 pounds, 22 year old Ruth Woolf was about to realize her childhood dream of having her own horse. Somehow, the dream of a horse was more enjoyable than the reality of a horse.

This horse, Pet, would be essential in realizing her second childhood dream: teaching in a rural school in a one room schoolhouse. Pet would be her transportation from the Soda Springs Ranch where she would be boarding to the Beaver Creek Schoolhouse, three miles away. Ruth had never owned a horse and until three days ago, had never ridden one. In her first riding experience she had gone on a cattle drive which left her a bit shaken and very sore. Today's ride would be a "trial run" to see how long it would take her to get to school and for David and Virginia to point out prob-

Ruth with "Pet," photo courtesy of Sedona Heritage Museum.

lems she might encounter on the trail. Ruth had already made a somewhat scandalous decision. She was not about to ride side saddle in her skirt as many young ladies did. She had a split leather skirt she would use to ride to school then change in to a more "teacher appropriate" gingham skirt. Her pay would be 50.00 a month.

The three miles between the ranch and school seemed like two very different worlds. Soda Springs was a working ranch on Beaver Creek. A green oasis, with huge Cottonwood and Sycamore trees, sweet smelling air and lush undergrowth. Many animals called it home. Birds, deer, rabbits lived along the banks. Fish of all kinds, beavers and otters swam in the river. The Finnie family, like many ranchers, had turned their working cattle ranch into a "dude" ranch. People from the east could come and "play" cowboy, ride horses, "help" with cattle and go on trail rides. The guests could sleep in the bunk house and eat delicious meals served family style in the dining room. After a hard day of playing cowboy they could swim in the soda springs pool. The soda content in the pool was so high guests "bobbed around like corks." After dinner there was singing under the stars around the campfire with the cowboys leading the singing while strumming their guitars. Ruth was indeed

fortunate to board at Soda Springs Ranch. Traveling a few hundred yards

Children arriving at school on a burro. Photo courtesy of Sedonda Heritage Museum.

Neighboring communities came together to play a baseball game, 1920's, courtesy of Sedona Heritage Museum.

away from the creek up the hills the ground turned into loose sand, rocks and white limestone with scant vegetation. The air was hot and dry. There were wild animals as well. Rattlesnakes, lizards, scorpions, roadrunners and jackrabbits. Coyotes prowled around, their eerie howling could often be heard in the distance. The school was adequate with a wood burning stove, chalkboard, desks for the children, big windows and one piece of playground equipment—a maypole.

Her first day of teaching school she found she had 20 students ages ranging from kindergarten to boys 15 and 16. Many of the male students were considerably taller than she. The older boys were often years behind in their schooling for

Children playing with the maypole at Beaver Creek School, Courtesy of Sedona Hertiage Museum.

lack of a teacher at the school or unable to attend because they were needed on the ranch.

Ruth may have been small, but she quickly established herself as the authority in the classroom and her students were always respectful, grateful for the opportunity to go to school. It didn't take long for Ruth to fall in love with her horse, Pet. Each day she put her skirt in a flour sack, loaded up her lunch, water and teaching supplies and rode three miles to school. Upon arriving Ruth went to the outhouse where she changed into her skirt. She built a fire in the wood-stove when necessary.

Her pupils came from ranching families in the area. Most of them were eking out a living in the formidable land. She noticed that many had lice and did not wash or groom their hair in any way. One day Ruth confided in her friend Virginia her concerns, "They are just so unkempt." Virginia replied, "There must be a reason. Why don't you ask them?" Ruth did ask and was shocked to hear that these children were in this condition because there was no water available to them at their ranches. Ruth was now ready to remedy the situation. Tuesday became "wash day." Each of the girls had their hair washed and curled. The boy's hair was washed and cut. Lice treatment was also administered to those who needed it.

One of the things Ruth loved was putting on plays. One of the plays, Miss Wiggs of the Cabbage Patch was a favorite for Ruth and her students. The problem was there were more parts for girls than boys. How in the world could she get the boys to play girl parts? One morning she said, "A girl can play a boy without any problem, but it is VERY difficult for a boy to play a girl. I don't know if any of you boys think you might be good enough to try out for the girls' parts." Ruth had all her parts for the play filled in no time!

During recess Ruth joined in with a variety of games the children always wanted to play. Baseball, red rover, tag and many more burned off the excess energy. One day Ruth got wind that the students were planning on playing "hooky". She joined in the fun, saying they would all play hooky together and took all of the children to nearby Montezuma Castle for the day, where they enjoyed learning about the prehistoric Indian ruins and having a delicious picnic lunch. Ruth may have started what we now call "field trips".

Another treat for the students was each one got to do an

over-night at Soda Springs Ranch. Oh, how the students loved going there! Ruth became alarmed when one little boy at dinner was on his third helping. Ruth said, "I'm a little worried that you might get sick." He looked up at her and said, "Oh Miss Woolf, it feels so good to be full."

Usually the trips to and from school were an enjoyable and relaxing time for Ruth and Pet. One eventful afternoon she came upon a rattlesnake. Ruth was so terrified she began to throw rocks at the snake. After hitting it with at least 100 rocks and making sure it was dead, she went over and looked at her accomplishment. She could hardly wait to tell the cowboys back at the ranch what she had done. "They will never believe me," she thought. So she picked up the snake and tied it to the saddle horn and brought it back to the ranch. The fact that Pet did not go berserk is a testimony to his good nature. Horses hate snakes. Arriving at the ranch, she dismounted and drug the snake to where the cowboys were working. They looked at her in disbelief. One said, "We might have believed you would kill a snake, but we NEVER would have thought you would bring it home!"

Walter and Ruth on their honeymoon at the Grand Canyon, 1930. Photo courtesy of Sedona Heritage Museum.

The school served as the center of community life as well. Dances were held, town meetings and potlucks or dessert socials. One evening the young adults from Verde Baptist Church in Cottonwood came to perform. Ruth was friends with one of them, Stella Jordan who she knew from her years at Tempe Normal School. Stella introduced Ruth to her brother, Walter. Walter and Ruth hit it off and the next week, Walter returned to take Ruth driving in his new Model A.

After a brief courtship Walter and Ruth married. Walter wanted to wait until November when all the harvesting was done, but Ruth did not want to spend another hot summer in Tempe. So in 1930 on July 23 at 5:30 a.m., the only bearable time of day, Walter and Ruth were married.

Walter and Ruth with Ruthie in their orchard . Photo courtesy of Sedona Heritage Museum.

They spent their honeymoon at the Grand Canyon. For many years Walter had longed for his own orchard. His brother George had taken interest in a parcel of land in the tiny community of Sedona. An adjoining parcel was available so Walter set a claim on it. There was much work to do to transform raw arid land into a working orchard. Walter did all his own grafting of young fruit

Ruthie, Anne and Walter "Sonny" at play, circa 1940. Photo courtesy of Sedona Heritage Museum.

trees, "so I can be sure what I am getting". He made a cage out of chicken wire and placed them around each small tree to protect from varmints. An orchard takes several years to grow before they start producing fruit. So vegetables were planted between the rows of trees. Carrots paid the bills in the early years. Pulled, bunched and boxed they were packed in a work truck and driven to Phoenix. Ruth helped with all aspects of the growing and harvesting process. She joined Walter on the six hour drive to Phoenix.

Walter with his two girls, 1935. Photo courtesy of Sedona Heritage Museum.

Ruth enjoyed this time with Walter. Then rather suddenly deliveries at the restaurants in Phoenix were difficult for Ruth. The smells of breakfast cooking and garbage at the back doors left her nauseous and sick. She found out she was pregnant.

For the next 5 years Ruth was preoccupied with her growing family. Anne was born in 1933, Ruthie one year later, in 1934 and Walter Jr., "Sonny" in 1936. Those years were particularly difficult for the Jordans with the depression affecting them and everyone else they knew. As the orchard grew and prospered the trees grew to the point that Walter's produce-rows were now shaded. Walter and Ruth talked it over. "The vegetable garden adds so much to the income," Walter told Ruth. "I hate to lose it. There are 55 acres for sale. Do you think we should buy it?" The cost of the land was $950.00. The Jordan's took a gamble, took out a loan and made the purchase. Walter planted Kentucky Wonder pole beans and had such a tremendous harvest he paid off the loan in one year.

In 1938 and 1939, Ruth spent summers attending summer school at Arizona State Teachers College in Flagstaff to further her education. They lived in Cottage City on campus. She took all three children with her and it was a marvelous time for the family. Ruth taught again during World War II. Her daughter Ruthie remembers well the year her mother taught at Red Rock School. She had 8 students from 1st grade to 8th grade. "It was the most wonderful year. I never had a year in which I learned so much. My Mother taught us everything; science, math, and biology. She made learning fun."

Orchards are labor intensive and difficult anywhere but Arizona has its own particular problems. The biggest problem is that northern Arizona is at the southernmost end of the Rocky Mountain Range. Spring can be cold and unpredictable. Frost is always a serious threat. Ruth explained that, "In forty-two years, only one year we didn't smudge." The smudging was difficult for the whole Jordan family and any hired hands.

One year Walter panicked as he watched the temperature fall precipitously in the evening. At about 11 p.m. Walter ran into the house to get Ruth who had already retired to bed. "I need to start smudging right now, I can't do this alone, go see if you can find some help" Since there were no telephones in Sedona at the time "rounding up help" meant physically going from door to door. Ruth came up with a brilliant plan! She would go to Oak Creek Tavern, about a mile away, surely there would be some men there. Ruth didn't want to waste time changing clothes so she went dressed as she was. Ruth always wore a cap to bed to keep her head warm. On this particular night the cap was bright red wool. She had on her flannel pajamas, knee socks pulled up over her pajama legs with a wool scarf

---

<u>Smudging at the Jordan Orchard</u> (courtesy of the Sedona Heritage Museum)

As soon as the buds on the trees began to swell, Walter kept an "eagle eye" on the weather. He kept meticulous records and compared current conditions with the past. He also knew local conditions, i.e., that the wind from the northeast was colder than from the northeast which was tempered by moving across Oak Creek. At the right time of the year, all the smudge pots were set in the orchards, filled with fuel, and dampers opened and cleaned. When smudging was imminent or in progress, three side-by-side thermometers were checked regularly during the night. Also, a drop of water on a saucer was watched to see if a skim of ice was forming. Knowing the killing temperature for each stage of a blossom, Walter could gauge when the heaters had to be lighted and how many degrees to raise the orchard's temperature. He also knew that there was a wide variance of temperature from one part of the ranch to the other.

<u>The Weather Station</u>

Ruth would check the thermometers hourly during the early part of the night, but as it grew colder, the alarm was set for every 30 minutes. Many times the thermometer would see-saw up and down just above the danger mark so Walter would get a full night's sleep and Ruth very little. Eventually Walter devised a thermostat that ran on batteries and was tied to a buzzer beside his bed.

78

Anne on left, Homecoming Queen at Cottonwood High School, 1949. Courtesy of Sedona Heritage Museum.

pinned to her neck. She had donned a half-length blue robe. As she went outside she topped this off with a shorter pink robe. She added Walter's heavy red and black Mackinaw (wool hat) and gloves. She jumped into the work truck and drove the mile to the tavern. When Ruth Jordan rushed into the Oak Creek Tavern every man there thought they had one too many drinks. Later, when Walter saw her come home in that attire he said, "Ruth, I can't believe you went like that." She replied, "I got two men to come help you didn't I?"

The orchard and children continued to grow. The two daughters were local beauties.

In the early 50's Ruth decided it was time to have a new kitchen. She hired a local pastor that did carpentry on the side. He brought along his two sons to help. The kitchen turned out to be the marvel and talk of all Sedona. Modern with many new innovations and many gadgets to help Ruth and accommodate her short stature. By the end of the remodel, Ruth and Walter also had two son-in-laws. In 1952, Anne married Robert Jackson and in 1954, Ruthie married Larry Jackson.

Walter and Ruth continued to operate their very successful orchard business, 120 acres of apples and peaches until 1973. At one time, they were the largest single employer in Sedona. Now in their mid-

Ruth and Walter working together into their later years, holding hands coming out of their packing shed. Photo courtesy of Sedona Heritage Museum.

seventies the orchard business was becoming too difficult to manage. At the same time Sedona was changing from a sleepy little town into a tourist haven and desirable place to retire. Walter and Ruth began selling their land. They kept the house, packing shed and a good amount of land which they enjoyed the remainder of their lives.

Life facts
Walter Jordan 1897-1987
Ruth Woolf Jordan 1902-1996
Children
Ann 1933-2010
Ruthie 1934
Walter "Sonny" 1936

Grandchildren: 7

Epilogue

Today the home of the Sedona Heritage Museum is in the Jordan Historical Park in the Jordan family's historic home and orchard buildings. The museum opened October 18, 1998. Daily the museum host visitors from around the world including hundreds of school children for educational experiences. Hundreds of other guests come for special events, programs, research or to tour the home and grounds. Walter and Ruth's original one room cabin is in the center of the home and has been restored with family artifacts. The iconic 1950's kitchen remains much the same and is a visitor favorite. One room is restored as Ruth's classroom in her days at Beaver Creek School. The Sedona Heritage museum focuses primarily on how our early pioneers lived, cattle ranching, the orchard industry and the almost 100 feature motion pictures and many television shows that were made in Sedona. The museum is located at:

735 Jordan Road, in Uptown Sedona.

Open Daily, 11-3. 928-282-7038 www.sedonamuseum.org

The Jordan's home now the Sedona Heritage Museum. Photo courtesy of Sedona Heritage Museum.

The Sprinklers, September 1967

Verner G. Benson

*Author's Note: It is a bit of thin thread that connects Ruth Jordan to "The Sprinklers." It may be my best chance though to include it in a book. It is one of my favorite stories of the 35+ stories that my Dad wrote. He went on to write two more humorous stories about NAU.

One of the more intriguing spectator sports at Northern Arizona University (NAU) owes its existence not to the athletic department, but to the department of buildings and grounds. That is the department responsible for the automatic sprinkler system which helps keep NAU green. Each segment of the system is controlled by a clock. At a pre-selected time the clock turns on the water for 4 to 10 minutes.

These clocks are set with diabolical cunning. One can almost see grounds department people pouring over the timing plans by the light of a flickering candle, chuckling. Clocks are never set to open during the time classes are changing, thereby eliminating a mob of irate students, mad as wet hens (used here both metaphorically and literally), descending upon the grounds department. They are timed, rather, to catch the malcontents, students late to class, young ladies dallying with boy friends not their own, hurrying professors hoping to get to class before the 10 minutes waiting period expires with fears of arriving exactly 10 minutes late and being left bloody and broken in the doorway in wake of the students' mad rush to escape. These are the victims, indignant but held to silence by the knowledge that speech will only bring exposure.

Sprinklers always give a short warning before coming on. Hisses, gurgles and low groans give evidence that water is forcing the air from the lines. There is usually ample time to escape, but the victim stands transfixed, much as a bird hypnotized by a snake. One second's hesitations and all is lost.

A psychiatrist, if he could stay calm and dry, could learn a great deal about people under stress. Old hands always enter the sprinkler areas with a great deal of caution. New students enter without caution and emerge without permanent waves.

When caught in the sprinklers people react differently. Women tend to react in accordance with the area in their formative years were spent. Girls from small towns attempt to hold down their skirts and giggle. Girls from large cities attempt to protect their hair and giggle. Older girls from both cities and towns attempt to hold down their skirts and protect their hair but very few have been observed to giggle.

Men, on the other hand, tend to react in accordance with their major subject. Forestry majors stride through the sprinklers, heads high, ignoring the elements. English ma-

Love defeated

Love triumphant

jors compose poetry. (At least they appear to be composing poetry. Their brows are furrowed, apparently in concentration, and their lips are moving.) Physical education majors run. This gives them an athletic appearance, unless they happen to hit a slick spot on the sidewalk. Music majors practice voice. It is odd, however, that they all seem to pick the same aria, you know, the one that starts – EEEEEOOOOOWWWW Possibly from "Carmen."

Teachers seem to react in accordance with rank. Instructors throw caution to the wind and bolt. Assistant professors, torn between dignity and the very human desire to stay dry, walk 10 steps, run 10 steps. Full professors smile wistfully, puzzled by rain that comes from below. Deans always look around for a likely student to blame it on, tarry too long and catch cold.

The clocks are set to turn on the sprinklers twice in 24 hours. For example, that sprinkler which doused the freshman carrying $65 worth of new textbooks during the noon hour will come on again shortly after midnight to flush lovers from the bushes by water of a crackling 40 degrees. And the sprinkler which wets the lawns around the Union Building at midmorning will douse a well-dressed concert audience at night.

In general, however, the night games are pretty dull. Only in the daytime do you see a young lady sunbathing atop what she believes is a rock. It is actually a sprinkler head capable of discharging 30 gallons of water per minute.

And only in the daytime do you see an art class setting up its easels on the lawn, chatting happily, unaware that in one minute and 37 seconds a bank of sprinklers will go on.

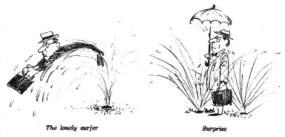

The lonely surfer

Surprise

Acknowledgements

Clara Brown
I first heard about Clara Brown while visiting the Ouray County Museum in Ouray, Colorado. It was over 20 years ago, but I still remember her story. It was inspiring! Books: "Aunt Clara Brown: Story of a Black Pioneer", Kathleen Bruyn, Pruett Publishing Co. 1970. "One More Mountain, One more Valley, the Story of Aunt Clara Brown", Linda Lowery, Random House, 2002. Thanks to my talented son-in law, Joe Blalock, Jr. for his sketch of Clara Brown.

Sally Rooke
Thanks to Roger Sanchez, director of the Raton Museum for directing me to local heroine, Sally Rooke. It is a wonderful museum in the delightful town of Raton, New Mexico. Thanks to Joe Blalock, Jr. for his sketch of Sally Rooke.

Mary Ann Tewksbury
I am happy to report the charisma that characterized the original four Tewksbury brothers is very much alive in their descendants four and five generations later! Thanks to great-grandsons of Mary Ann, Bill Brown (Bertha) and John Rhodes (John Tewksbury) grand-daughter, Mary Bryce (Nan) and great- grand-daughter of Edwin Tewksbury, Barbara Tewksbury. I enjoyed immensely the delightful conversations about Mary Ann, the family and the Pleasant Valley War. I believe I first heard about the Pleasant Valley War when I was a freshman at NAU in 1970. I had a class with Bernie Tewksbury from Globe. The whole semester she thrilled me with stories of her heritage. I don't remember the class or anything I learned in that class, but I never forgot Bernie! Thanks to Wilma Haught for her valuable information, photos and tour of the Perkins Store Museum, in Young, Arizona. The museum was once the home of Mary Ann and her family. Thanks to Donna Anderson of the Gila County Museum in Globe, Arizona for an abundance of information and photos. Books: "A Little War of Our Own", Don Dedera, Northland Press, Flagstaff, Arizona 1988. "Pleasant Valley War", Jinx Pyle, Git a Rope! Publishing Inc., Payson, Arizona 2009.

Pearl Cromer
Thanks to Mike and Sarah Cromer for their remberance of Mike's grandmother. I enjoyed the wonderful conversations over coffee or Mexican food. Their enthusiasm, appreciation and encouragement is greatly appreciated. Thanks to Donna Anderson, Gila County Museum in Globe, Arizona for help with the history of Globe and the story, "The First Christmas in Globe."

Veronica Michelbach
Thanks to Marilyn Michelbach Coy for her wonderful story about her grandmother. It was great to reminisce about growing up in Flagstaff and the long, warm history between the Michelbach and Benson Families.

Ruth Jordan
Thanks to Ruth Van Epps for her remembrance of her mother, Ruth Jordan. Thanks to Janeen Trevillyan and the Sedona Historical Society for use of their

research facility, photos, and additional information. Books:
"Following Their Westward Star", Jordan Ruth, Moore Graphics Surprise,
Arizona, 2005.

Thanks to Stephanie Goodwin for transcribing all of my dad's stories from the
original published copies to the computer.

Thanks to my wonderful editor, Randi Diskin. She can do everything I can't!
A teacher by profession she is also a photographer, a techy, a computer whiz,
graphic designer and she DRIVES! Plus she is lots of fun, a great encourager
and the most pleasant person to spend time with. Thank you Randi, I would be
lost without you!